# Seo

## How to Build a Successful Handmade Business

*(The Proven Guide to Start Run and Grow a Successful Consulting Business)*

**Philip Barber**

Published By **Phil Dawson**

# Philip Barber

*Seo: How to Build a Successful Handmade Business (The Proven Guide to Start Run and Grow a Successful Consulting Business)*

ISBN   978-1-7781960-7-2

No part of this guidebook shall be reproduced in any form without permission in writing from the publisher except in the case of brief quotations embodied in critical articles or reviews.

Legal & Disclaimer

The information contained in this book is not designed to replace or take the place of any form of medicine or professional medical advice. The information in this book has been provided for educational & entertainment purposes only.

The information contained in this book has been compiled from sources deemed reliable, and it is accurate to the best of the Author's knowledge; however, the Author cannot guarantee its accuracy and validity and cannot be held liable for any errors or omissions. Changes are periodically made to this book. You must consult your doctor or get professional medical advice before using any of the suggested remedies, techniques, or information in this book.

Table Of Contents

# Chapter 1: Understanding Search Engines

2.1. How Do Search Engines Work?

Let's take a bit journey into the coronary coronary heart of a are seeking out engine. You've probable used one like Google or Bing infinite times, however have you ever questioned how they control to find out precisely what you are searching out in a break up 2nd? Well, it is all down to 3 number one steps: Crawling, Indexing, and Ranking. Let's spoil it down.

1. Crawling:

So accept as true with the internet as a huge city and the search engines like google as explorers. The explorers start their journey by using sending out scouts, called 'crawlers' or 'spiders' (do not worry, the ones spiders are quality!). These digital critters have an unmarried project: to roam the city, popping into every constructing (internet site) they may be capable of discover and finding out what is interior.

They test the whole lot from textual content and photos to movement images and the underlying code that holds all of it together. They're thorough, and that they do no longer leave out a element. They even use the town's delivery links (or the hyperlinks on a net web site) to move round.

2. Indexing:

After the crawlers have toured the town and stated everything down, they head again home and record their findings. This information is then stored in a huge digital library known as the 'index'.

Think of the index because the seek engine's personal encyclopedia of the internet. It's in which they maintain a reproduction of every constructing (internet website) they've visited. However, not each constructing makes it to the index. Some might be too run-down (horrible extraordinary content fabric cloth), while others is probably breaking the town's pointers (seek engine pointers).

three. Ranking:

Now, at the same time as you type a search into Google, what you are really doing is calling the search engine to sift via its extensive encyclopedia and find out the maximum relevant entries for you. The searching for engine ranks those entries in what it believes to be the order of relevance and price, and provides them to you as seek results.

The are seeking engine desires to provide you with the high-quality feasible answer to your query, and so it makes use of a mystery recipe (set of guidelines) to determine the order of the effects. The recipe takes underneath interest masses of substances (rating factors), some of which we're going to be revealing in the following couple of chapters.

In a nutshell, search engines like google like google like google and yahoo are like tireless explorers, continuously traveling through the net, making notes, and providing you with the high-quality viable solutions in your questions. Understanding how they do that is the first step to growing your website more appealing to them (and to your visitors). Stick round, because of the fact we are without a doubt getting started out out on this search engine optimization journey!

## 2.2. Search Engine Algorithms: What You Need to Know

Alright, it is time to talk approximately some difficulty that could sound a bit intimidating inside the starting - are seeking for engine algorithms. But do not worry! We're going to break it down and make it as first-class as viable.

So, what is a looking for engine set of guidelines? Well, recollect you are at a celebration with hundreds of people, and you are searching out your pal, Sam. How must you discover him? You'd probably begin by way of asking some questions, proper? What does he seem like? What's he sporting? Who is he probable to be speaking to?

Search engine algorithms perform a little component comparable. When a person types in a are searching for question, the quest engine desires to find out the maximum relevant and useful records to show them, just like you want to locate Sam on the celebration. To do this, it asks its non-public set of questions about every website it is aware of. These questions might probably encompass:

How relevant is this website to the hunt query?

How popular is that this net internet website online?

How authoritative and sincere is it?

The way the hunt engine asks and weighs those questions is its set of guidelines.

Now, are looking for engine algorithms aren't static. They're like chameleons, constantly converting and adapting to offer clients the wonderful possible consequences. Google, as an example, is thought to make hundreds of adjustments to its set of guidelines each year! That's why seek engine marketing is not a 'set it and overlook it' shape of element. It requires non-forestall reading and version.

So, how are we able to probable maintain up with the ones ever-changing algorithms? The proper facts is, you do now not want to apprehend every tiny detail. Phew! The most crucial element to preserve in mind is that this: serps like google and yahoo like google intention to offer the fantastic possible consequences for their users.

That method in case you recognition on growing great, relevant content and offering an notable man or woman revel in, you are already on the proper song. Search engines will understand and praise your efforts.

In the subsequent chapters, we are going to dive deeper into how you can optimize your net web web site to align with the ones algorithmic requirements. So, allow's keep this search engine advertising party going!

2.Three. The Role of seek engine advertising in Digital Marketing

This time, we are going to dive into the location of seo within the grand scheme of factors, in particular, digital advertising.

So, image digital advertising and marketing as a huge, bustling town. There are masses of various neighborhoods, each with its own vibe and attraction. You've have been given the Social Media district, with its contemporary cafes and non-forestall chatter. The Email Marketing vicinity is sort of a reliable antique buddy, continually there with a comforting ordinary. Pay-Per-Click (PPC) is the flashy, fast-paced downtown with neon lights and large crowds. And then, there's the seo community, a key a part of town that connects all of the others.

search engine marketing is similar to the infrastructure of our digital marketing town. It's the roads and highways that get human beings from component A to point B. Without it, the town might now not feature well. It permits guide site visitors (aka ability customers) to the proper places (your brilliant internet website online), and makes positive they have got a clean and thrilling adventure along the manner.

What's extra, seek engine advertising and advertising is like a town planner, normally thinking about the extended-term growth and improvement of the city. While a few advertising and marketing strategies may additionally offer you with quick wins, seo is all approximately sustainable achievement. It's a protracted exercise, but boy, is it absolutely well worth it!

With powerful seo, your internet site can rank higher in are seeking for engine outcomes, making it less tough for humans to find you. It can growth your visibility and credibility, power extra traffic for your website, and in the end, increase income and boom.

Sounds pretty incredible, right? But the excellent detail is, search engine marketing and the possibility virtual advertising and marketing and advertising and advertising and marketing strategies aren't together one-of-a-type. They can, and want to, paintings together in harmony. For example, the important thing phrases you operate for seek engine advertising and advertising additionally can be used on your PPC campaigns or social media posts to create a cohesive logo message.

So, in our virtual advertising and marketing metropolis, seek engine marketing isn't always only a network. It's the framework that holds the whole thing collectively. It's the grasp plan for achievement. And that, my pal, is why search engine optimization is the kind of huge deal in digital advertising. Let's hold our journey and find out more about this charming world!

Let's check yourself!

1. If engines like google were a grocery keep, what may want to the algorithms be?

a) The shopping for cart.

b) The grumpy safety defend.

c) The ultra-inexperienced shop manager organizing all the aisles and merchandise.

d) The unfastened samples stand.

2. What's the fine way to attraction the paranormal creatures referred to as are attempting to find engine algorithms?

a) Write them a heartfelt love letter.

b) Build a notable net internet site with applicable content material fabric, optimized key terms, and fantastic inbound links.

c) Send them a field of digital donuts.

d) All of the above (wishful thinking, we apprehend).

3. How do engines like google see web sites?

a) Through rose-coloured glasses.

b) As a delicious multi-layered virtual cake.

c) Through crawlers (moreover known as spiders or bots).

d) They truely decide upon audiobooks.

four. How does search engine optimization in form into the grand scheme of digital advertising?

a) It's just like the salsa to your nachos, bringing taste and zing in your on-line presence.

b) It's a whole separate global, like Narnia.

c) It's an essential tool for growing your internet site's visibility and the usage of natural traffic.

d) It's that cousin who suggests up uninvited to all circle of relatives sports.

5. What's the golden rule of seek engine advertising in virtual advertising and marketing?

a) Always put on a helmet.

b) Content is King.

c) When doubtful, dance it out.

d) There's no such component as an excessive amount of glitter.

Hey, consider to test your answers at the quit of the ebook!

## Chapter 2: Keywords

three.1. What are Keywords?

The Secret Ingredients inside the seek engine marketing Recipe!

So, you might be asking, "What within the international are key terms?" Well, let me will can help you understand, they will be loads much less tough than you might imagine. Picture this: you are seeking out a present day recipe for chocolate chip cookies.

You probable may not kind into Google, "How do I make a sweet circular dessert with little bits of chocolate internal?" No, you may probable search for "chocolate chip cookie recipe." And there you have got were given it, "chocolate chip cookie recipe" is your key-word!

In the massive worldwide of SEO, key phrases are the phrases or phrases that humans kind into serps like google and yahoo. They're the questions humans are asking, the offerings they are searching out, and the products they want to buy. And your hobby, as an search engine optimization magician, is to make sure your net website solutions those queries and appears at the same time as those key terms are searched. Easy peasy, proper?

But don't forget, it is now not pretty a awesome deal throwing as many key phrases as you may onto your web website and hoping for the great. No, no, no. Search engines are clever (recollect our talk approximately algorithms?), and they price great, relevant content. So, your key phrases need for use glaringly inner your content material material, offering charge and answering the questions your capability visitors are asking.

So, to sum all of it up, key phrases are the magic phrases that be a part of searchers together with your internet site. Choose them accurately, use them efficaciously, and watch as your internet site on-line climbs the quest engine rankings!

3.2. How to Find the Right Keywords?

Welcome decrease once more, my fellow search engine optimization adventurers! Now that we recognize what key terms are, it is time to embark on a interesting treasure hunt – the hunt for the proper key phrases. So, hold close your virtual shovels and allow's get digging!

So, how can we find out these golden nuggets of search engine optimization? Well, it's now not as complicated as it would appear. Picture your self as a detective, trying to get into the minds of the oldsters which are searching for the product, carrier, or facts that you're supplying. What phrases or phrases may also need to they type into the search engine? This is your location to begin.

But, as any correct detective is aware of, you can not in reality depend on your gut instinct. No, you want robust proof. And this is where key-word research equipment are to be had in available. These amazing system, like Google Keyword Planner, Ahrefs or SEMrush, can display you precisely what human beings are searching for, how often, and how much competition there may be for each keyphrase. It's like having your very very personal crystal ball!

Remember, the first-rate key terms are not usually the most searched for. They're those which might be maximum relevant on your content and feature the right stability of searching for amount and competition. So, don't be tempted through the vibrant appeal of immoderate-amount keywords if they are now not a brilliant fit on your net web site.

One extra tip in advance than we wrap up: endure in thoughts approximately prolonged-tail key phrases. These are longer, more unique terms that human beings could likely look for. They typically have decrease seek volumes, but additionally they've got lots much less competition and often motive better conversion expenses. So, they will be real hidden gems!

Short-tail keywords

typically one to two phrases and are very well-known. For instance:

1.      "Running shoes"

2.      "Pizza"

3.      "Laptop"

4.      "iPhone"

5.      "Coffee"

These key phrases have a tendency to have very immoderate attempting to find volumes, but they're additionally very competitive and not very particular, that can make it more difficult to rank for them and extra hard to draw the right audience.

Long-tail key phrases

They're longer phrases which are more precise. They usually have a propensity to have decrease are trying to find volumes, but they're also less aggressive and extra targeted, that may lead them to more effective for seo. Here are a few examples:

1.    "Best walking footwear for marathon schooling"

2.    "Gluten loose pizza delivery in Chicago"

3.    "Laptop with first-class battery lifestyles"

four.    "Refurbished iPhone 11 Pro Max"

5.    "Organic sincere change coffee beans"

By using long-tail key phrases, you may intention a more unique target market it honestly is much more likely to be interested by what you're imparting.

3.Three. Keyword Research Tools

So, my friend, you presently understand what key terms are and a manner to find out the right ones. But you're likely questioning, "Surely, there want to be a few magical gadget to assist me with this?" Well, you're in particular fortune! There are some great key-phrase research equipment available that will help you find out the ones hidden key-phrase gems. Let's get to recognize a number of them!

1.

Google Keyword Planner: It's just like the Hogwarts of key-phrase studies gadget! Google Keyword Planner is a loose device, and it's all approximately displaying you what people are looking for on Google. It gives you thoughts for logo spanking new key phrases, suggests how regularly key phrases are searched, and even indicates the volume of competition you could face for every key-word.

2.

SEMrush: SEMrush is sort of a Swiss Army Knife for SEO. This tool can offer you with specific data about key-word seek volumes, competition, and in addition. Plus, it is able to show you what key phrases your competition are using. It's like having your very own private are seeking for engine advertising secret agent!

3.

Moz Keyword Explorer: Moz's device is some other terrific assistant on your key-word studies adventure. It gives you key-word pointers, SERP (Search Engine Results Page) evaluation, and a key-word's are searching for quantity. It's like having a crystal ball which could expect your seek engine advertising future!

4.

Ubersuggest: Ubersuggest is just like the genie of key-phrase studies equipment. It generates extended-tail key-phrase thoughts for any issue count number and indicates you the top-ranking SERPs for them.

5.

AnswerThePublic: This device is like your non-public mind reader, displaying you what questions human beings are asking spherical your key-phrase. It's a awesome manner to locate lengthy-tail key terms and come up with content material material thoughts that at once solution your goal marketplace's questions.

6.

Ahrefs: Ahrefs is like your tremendous community detective, usually equipped to dig up useful insights about your net site's search engine advertising and marketing standard overall performance and your competition. It's your circulate-to pal for uncovering the excellent key phrases, finding out one manner hyperlinks, and essentially helping you turn out to be the superstar of search engine results.

Remember, every of those device has its private strengths and weaknesses, so it is properly worth attempting out a few to appearance which one suits your dreams exquisite. It's like attempting on footwear – you need to discover the one that fits really right!

Let's take the example of an internet store selling toys for dogs. By the usage of a mixture of quick and lengthy tail key phrases, along side 'canine toys', 'interactive toys for dogs', and 'squeaky toys for small dogs', the store can enchantment to greater capacity customers and boom their opportunities of making profits!

1.

Short tail keywords: canine toys, puppy toys, doggy toys, toys for puppies

("For" is a preposition and isn't normally covered as a key-word in are searching for engine advertising. Therefore, "toys for dog" may be considered a quick tail key-word because it consists of handiest terms)

2.

Long tail key terms: bite toys for puppies, squeaky toys for small puppies, plush toys for big dogs, difficult toys for aggressive chewers

3.

Branded key terms: Kong dog toys, Nylabone canine toys, Chuckit! Dog toys

4.

Geographic key phrases: canine toys UK, puppy toys USA, puppy toys Canada

5.

Action-orientated key terms: purchase canine toys online, order puppy toys, store for domestic dog toys

6.

Industry-associated key phrases: quality dog toys, green puppy toys, durable pup toys

7.

Related phrases: dog treats, canine beds, dog collars, canine grooming tool.

During keyword studies on your internet web site, bear in mind that you're now not likely to have all of them, at the least now not to begin with – besides your enterprise is exceedingly area of hobby. Focus on super in desire to quantity. Prioritize the maximum valuable key terms first and create an prolonged-term approach, consisting of walking a weblog, for the rest.

Aim for lengthy-tail key terms. Choosing fine quick-tail key phrases as a present day internet web page, you may not be capable of outrank set up sites that have built their positions over some years. Keep in thoughts that Google is sensible and is aware of variations and inflections. The plural form or inflected instances of your key-word aren't truly new keywords to Google!

I preference you're playing our journey into the world of seo as plenty as I am. Next up, we're going to dive right into a way to use the ones key phrases effectively. Stay tuned, my search engine marketing apprentice!

Let's test your self!

1.

What are key phrases inside the international of digital advertising and advertising?

a) Magic phrases that open mystery internet doors

b) The phrases you scream at your laptop at the same time because it freezes

c) The precise terms human beings use in serps to discover what they need

d) The phrases you kind right right into a searching for engine to get lost within the net

2.

Why is it essential to locate the proper key terms for your internet site?

a) To make your net internet web page look pretty

b) To make sure people can discover your net website even as they'll be looking on line

c) To confuse search engines and motive them to art work more tough

d) Because the internet advised you to

3.

Which of those is NOT a key-word studies device?

a) Google Keyword Planner

b) SEMRush

c) Microsoft Excel

d) Ahrefs

4.

Which of those isn't an outstanding way to find the right key terms?

a) Throwing a dart at a dictionary

b) Using Google's "People also ask" function

c) Researching what key phrases your competition are the usage of

d) Analyzing the key phrases that deliver net page website traffic on your very very personal web page

five.

What must you do after figuring out your aim key phrases?

a) Add them to your internet internet site online as tons as viable, although it makes the textual content unreadable

b) Forget about them and desire for the splendid

c) Use them strategically to your content material cloth and show their overall performance

d) There isn't always any need to discover key phrases

Hey, take into account to check your solutions on the prevent of the e-book!

4. On-Page seo

four.1. URL Structure

The Street Address of Your Webpage

Hey there, search engine advertising and marketing film movie star! Ready to dive into the interesting international of URL structures? Great! Now, sincerely as you would not need your property address to be a confusing mess, the same goes for your internet web site – it desires a clean, clean-to-understand URL shape.

URL, or Uniform Resource Locator, is simply a flowery way of announcing "net deal with." It's the particular set of instructions that factors the internet to the correct internet web page it desires to locate on your website. Think of it much like the GPS coordinates for every internet internet web page of your internet site on-line.

Now, you might be thinking, "Why does my URL form consider?" Well, similar to a neat and tidy avenue is less tough to navigate, a nicely-set up URL makes it much less complex for engines like google like Google to locate and apprehend your webpages. This can give you a leg up in search engine marketing scores, and who could no longer want that?

A nicely URL shape want to be logically prepared and without problems readable, each for the search engines like google and yahoo and for human beings. That manner maintaining off lengthy strings of numbers and gibberish. Instead, goal for short, descriptive, and key-word-rich URLs. For example:

www.Mywebsite.Com/excellent-chocolate-cake-recipe is a fantastic deal more appealing and informative than

www.Mywebsite.Com/post12345, proper?

And consider, virtually as you would not exchange your home deal with every unique day, try to avoid changing your URLs too regularly. This can result in damaged hyperlinks, and obtain as true with me, search engines like google and yahoo like google and yahoo do not like that. Plus, it could confuse your normal visitors.

In the subsequent sections, we'll dive deeper into how you can optimize your URL shape to create a tidy, navigable net internet site that every search engines like google and yahoo like google like google and yahoo and your internet site online visitors will respect. Stay tuned, due to the fact we're just getting started out out on this thrilling journey to appearance engine advertising mastery!

4.2. Meta Tags

## Chapter 3: The Invisible Heroes Of Seo

Imagine going to a e-book place (positive, those although exist!). Before you commit to a ebook, you have a look at the cover, possibly examine the precis at the lower again, or perhaps sneak a peek on the primary net page. Well, meta tags do a comparable hobby in your internet site. They offer search engines like google and customers a sneak peek of what your web page is all about while not having to dive deep into your content material.

"Wait, however I cannot see them!" you may possibly say. You're proper! Meta tags are like invisible stagehands in a play, doing all the hard work behind the scenes. They exist within the HTML of your internet site and speak important information approximately your net page to look engine bots.

There are precise kinds of meta tags, however the  large ones you need to understand approximately are the meta call and the meta description.

The meta call is the pick out out of your web web page that suggests up in looking for engine results. It's similar to the headline of a newspaper article – make it catchy and relevant to the content of the internet page (50-60 characters). It's a super idea to install writing the words within the name in capital letters to motive them to more seen to the person's eyes!

The meta description is a short summary that looks below the call in seek results. It's much like the blurb on the again of a e-book – it want to be compelling and supply a brief evaluation of what the vacationer can assume to locate to your internet web page (one hundred twenty-a hundred and fifty five characters).

When crafting your meta tags, bear in mind to embody your targeted key terms in reality - but no keyword stuffing! We want to play high-quality with search engines like google and yahoo like google and yahoo like google and yahoo and clients alike.

A relevant example:

Keyword: "most well-known canine Pawsitively Happy

Meta Description: Uncover the maximum famous canine toys that have our furry buddies wagging their tails in 2023! From durable bite toys to interactive puzzles. Check it out!

Remember, an splendid meta perceive and description should no longer satisfactory consist of the important thing-word but additionally be appealing to capability readers, giving them an top notch reason to click on on to your hyperlink within the trying to find outcomes. It's an wonderful concept to characteristic CTA (Call To Action) to your meta description – most often it's far brought at the stop: Check it out! / Click and study our article! / Buy now 50% off! / Watch our video in recent times! / See now!

4.Three. Content Optimization

Making Your Words Shine at the Web Stage!

Hey there, seo explorer! You're once more for more, and we couldn't be extra thrilled. Today, we're moving into the heart of seo: Content Optimization. If you have ever perplexed a way to make your content material cloth dazzle within the colourful lights of the internet, you're inside the proper vicinity!

Content Optimization is all approximately making your internet website online's content as attractive and useful as feasible — now not most effective on your readers, but furthermore for the ones hardworking are seeking for engine bots who're always on the hunt for top-notch content material.

So, how do you optimize your content material cloth? Imagine you are baking a cake. You'd need to use the remarkable substances, proper? Well, in this situation, your components are your key terms. Sprinkle them in some unspecified time in the future of your content material cloth however be careful not to overdo it. Your text should despite the fact that sound natural and tasty. No one likes a key-word-filled, unreadable cake - I suggest, content fabric material!

Next, think about the shape of your content material material. Break up huge chunks of textual content into smaller, chunk-sized portions. Use headings and subheadings (bear in thoughts to embody the ones key terms!) to make your content material smooth to navigate. It's like reducing your cake into neat, inviting slices.

Don't forget about about approximately photographs and films too! They add flavor and range to your content material. Just bear in mind to optimize them as well, the use of alt tags (little descriptions that tell serps like google what the photograph or video is prepared). It's like along with a label on your cake so all people is aware of what deliciousness to assume.

There's no difficult and fast rule for the tremendous sort of pix in an seo article. It is based totally upon at the duration of the content material cloth fabric and the topic. Some posts might be fine with simply one or images, on the identical time as others, in particular longer or more complicated posts, might also additionally gain from more seen aids. What's vital is that each photograph provides value to the content material cloth, is well optimized with alt textual content for are looking for engine marketing, and does no longer sluggish down your internet page loading pace.

Finally, ensure your content material material is smooth and up to date. Regularly updating your content material is like generally having a clean cake prepared on your site visitors. Search engines love clean content cloth material, and so do your site visitors!

Remember, at the coronary coronary heart of content material optimization is the purpose to offer price on your readers. When your readers are happy, engines like google like google are glad too.

Remember! The period of the content fabric can vary extensively, however a not unusual recommendation is at least 3 hundred phrases for a easy blog positioned up or article. However, in-depth articles, publications, or property that intention to cowl a topic comprehensively is probably masses longer, even up to 2000 phrases or extra. It's important to provide in-intensity, precious information and now not absolutely add fluff to reap a pleasing phrase rely range.

Grab a cheat sheet!

1.

Choose Your Star: Identify the primary key-phrase for your content material material material. This keyword need to be the superstar of your display, reflecting the principle subject matter of your content material fabric fabric.

2.

Set the Stage: Include your key-phrase in your headline, ensuring it's miles catchy and applicable. This is your first chance to seize your target audience's interest, so make it rely!

3.

Make a Grand Entrance: Try to use your key-word within the first a hundred-one hundred fifty terms of your content material. This allows every your readers and are searching for engine bots understand what your content cloth is about proper from the get-skip.

4.

Perform Naturally: Use your keywords definitely throughout your content material. Remember to moreover use synonyms of your key-word. A top rule of thumb is to aim for a key-phrase density of about 1-2%. That way your key-word need to appear extra or a whole lot less five-10 instances in a 500-phrase article. But recollect, do now not overdo it – the text ought to despite the fact that have a look at certainly!

5.

Break a Leg: Break up your content material (at least 3 hundred phrases!) into digestible chunks with headings and subheadings. Bonus elements if you could obviously encompass your key-phrase in a number of those!

6.

Add Some Drama: Include relevant images or movement photos to beautify your content fabric cloth . Don't overlook approximately to use key-word-wealthy alt tags to describe them!

7.

Keep the Show Running: Regularly replace your content material to keep it glowing and applicable. Search engines and your audience love new fabric.

eight.

Take a Bow: End with a robust conclusion that summarizes your content material material. If feasible, try to encompass your key-word right right here too (remaining one hundred phrases), but excellent if it suits really.

9.

Connect the Dots: Incorporate internal and outdoor hyperlinks to your content fabric fabric to offer extra rate for your readers. For inner hyperlinks, manual your readers to different applicable content fabric material in your net web page. For outdoor hyperlinks, element them toward authoritative property that assist or increase upon your elements. Remember, the anchor textual content of your hyperlinks need to be descriptive and relevant to the associated content material fabric fabric. If it suits truely, you may even use your key-word inside the anchor text. But most importantly, every link need to provide a few component valuable to your reader. It's all about developing an internet of records that your reader will discover useful and appealing.

## Chapter 4: Using Keywords Effectively

The trick with key phrases isn't definitely to sprinkle them willy-nilly during your content fabric. Like a maintain near chef, you need to use them strategically. Here are some tips to guide you:

1.

Title Tag: Use your key-phrase on your pick out tag. This is the headline that shows up in are looking for engine effects. It's the number one detail human beings (and serps) see, so make it remember!

2.

Meta Description: This is the quick precis that looks below the call tag in are in search of engine outcomes. Including your key-phrase right here can help search engines like google like google and yahoo understand your content material fabric fabric, and it could additionally assist enchantment to readers.

three.

URL: If feasible, encompass your keyword for your URL. It's each different location search engines like google and yahoo like google appearance to recognize what your internet internet page is prepared.

4.

Headings and Subheadings: Including your key-word in as a minimum one heading and subheading can be useful. It allows split your content material fabric and makes it much less complicated for readers (and search engines like google and yahoo like google like google and yahoo) to recognize.

five.

In the Content: Use your key-word evidently inside the course of your content cloth cloth. Remember, the purpose isn't to stuff your content material with key phrases. Instead, aim for a herbal go with the flow that makes enjoy in your readers.

Long-Tail Keywords

Here's a touch insider tip for you: don't forget about long-tail key phrases! These are longer, greater unique phrases that humans could in all likelihood search for. For instance, in choice to "dog toys," an extended-tail key-phrase is probably "maximum well-known canine toys for massive breeds." Long-tail key phrases may be less aggressive and allow you to gather a extra centered intention market.

The Importance of Keywords

You is probably thinking, "Why are key terms so critical in search engine optimization?" Well, keep in mind this: whilst you're hungry for pizza, you do not clearly search for "meals," proper? You search for "top notch pizza close to me" or "pepperoni pizza recipe." The terms you operate are the key phrases, the guideposts that lead you to the records you need. They're further crucial to content material fabric creators and serps like google and yahoo, assisting to attach the proper content fabric cloth with the proper target marketplace.

More on Using Keywords Effectively

Let's have a have a look at keyword utilization a chunk more cautiously. We've mentioned the crucial thing locations you should encompass your keywords, just like the name tag, meta description, URL, headings, and within the content material fabric itself. But how do you do that effectively? Here are a few greater tips:

First a hundred-a hundred fifty terms: Try to embody your key-word in the first 100-150 phrases of your content. This permits search engines fast decide the subject of your content material material.

Last one hundred words: Similarly, using your key-word inside the course of the give up of your content material can aid its essential subject matter.

Keyword Frequency: While it is crucial to encompass key phrases in the direction of your content fabric material, keep away from "key-word stuffing." That's while you overuse your key-word, making your content material fabric cloth sound unnatural. This can absolutely harm your seek engine advertising and marketing as search engines like google and yahoo like google and yahoo like google choose content material cloth it truly is written for humans, no longer bots.

Synonyms and Variations: Use synonyms and variations of your key-phrase to cowl extra ground. For instance, if your key-word is "healthful dog food," variations can also need to embody "nutritious dog food," "dog food for fitness," or "wholesome dog diet regime."

Long-Tail Keywords and User Intent

We touched on lengthy-tail key phrases in advance, however they will be so important that they deserve a piece greater interest. These longer, greater specific key-word terms may be beneficial in project a more focused target audience and better matching character motive.

User cause is largely what the searcher is honestly searching out when they kind in a query. For instance, if a person searches for "satisfactory dog food for a Labrador," they're likely seeking out product suggestions or opinions. By the usage of this prolonged-tail key-phrase, you can create content material fabric that proper now addresses this motive.

And it's far a wrap on key phrases, dad and mom! Remember, the use of key terms efficaciously is like which include clearly the right quantity of spice to your stew – it makes the entirety come together fantastically. Happy keywording, and spot you inside the subsequent monetary disaster!

four.Five. Image Optimization

Ready to add a sprint of coloration in your seek engine advertising and marketing journey? That's proper, it is time to speak about picture optimization! Just like the proper GIF need to make a tweet pop, the proper photo can make your net internet web page extra attractive and extraordinary.

But did  that your pix can also play a function for your seek engine advertising and marketing and advertising approach? Let's dive in!

Why Bother with Image Optimization?

Images can do greater than certainly make your website look accurate. When nicely optimized, they also can make contributions to your website's visibility in are looking for engine results. How, you ask? By improving net web page load instances, improving man or woman enjoy, and providing search engines with more context about your web page's content.

Size Matters

First subjects first, allow's talk approximately period. No, no longer the scale of the photograph, but its file duration. Large photograph documents can slow down your net website online, and a sluggish-loading internet site can ship visitors bouncing lower again to the quest results faster than a kangaroo on a trampoline.

To keep away from this, it's an excellent concept to compress your pics in advance than uploading them on your internet web site. There are plenty of unfastened on line device that let you with this, like TinyPNG or CompressJPEG.

The Right Format

Next, remember the format of your photo. The maximum not unusual codecs are JPEG, PNG, and GIF.

JPEGs are awesome for pics or photos with loads of colours.

PNGs are perfect for pictures that require transparency, like logos.

GIFs are your skip-to for animations.

Choose the handiest that suits your desires even as keeping document size in thoughts.

Descriptive File Names

Here's a pro tip: in advance than importing an picture, deliver its report a descriptive call. For example, as opposed to "IMG_1234.Jpg", you could use "golden_retriever_puppy.Jpg". This can assist engines like google recognize what the picture is ready, and it may additionally assist your picture appear in image are searching for for outcomes.

Alt Text: The seek engine advertising Secret Weapon

Alt textual content (short for alternative text) is a brief description of an picture, which is displayed if the photo cannot be loaded and is observe through display readers for visually impaired clients. From an seek engine advertising and advertising attitude, alt textual content offers search engines with useful information about the image.

When writing alt text, try and be descriptive and, if it suits truly, encompass your key-word.

Caption This

While now not as crucial as alt textual content for seo, picture captions can be have a look at through search engines like google and yahoo like google and may assist provide context. Plus, human beings have a tendency to examine captions after they take a look at thru content material, so a first rate caption can assist interact your readers.

And there you've got were given it – the colourful international of picture optimization! Remember, every photo for your net website online is an possibility to improve your search engine marketing and create a higher consumer experience. So, skip on and make your internet website online photograph-best! See you within the next financial spoil.

## 4.6. Mobile-Friendly Design

Because seek engine advertising and marketing isn't Just a Desktop Affair

Hello again! Time to pocket that mouse, unplug that keyboard, and whip out your smartphones. Today, we are speaking approximately cellular-high-quality layout. In a international in which human beings Google from mountaintops and tweet from subways, making sure your net internet site appears incredible and competencies nicely on cellular devices is extra essential than ever. Let's dive into why this subjects and the manner you may hold close it!

Why Mobile-Friendly Design Matters

First matters first: why want to you care approximately mobile-exceptional design? Well, for starters, greater than half of of of all net site visitors now comes from cell gadgets. That's pretty some functionality visitors! Moreover, search engines like google and yahoo like google like google and yahoo like Google have started out out to use cellular-first indexing.

This approach they predominantly use the cellular model of your content for indexing and rating. So, if your internet web page isn't always mobile-exquisite, it's far not just your users you are letting down - it is also your seo.

What is Mobile-Friendly Design?

Mobile-fine layout, additionally referred to as responsive format, method your net website online adjusts to look precise and characteristic nicely on any tool, be it a computer, a tablet, or a phone. This consists of smooth navigation, speedy load instances, readable textual content, and easy-to-tap buttons, amongst various matters.

The ABCs of Making Your Site Mobile-Friendly

Now, let's see a few key factors of a cell-friendly layout:

1.

Easy-to-Read Content: On a smaller show, clarity is critical. Make powerful your textual content is massive sufficient to take a look at with out squinting or zooming. Break up your content material into smaller chunks with headings and bullet factors to make it more digestible.

2.

Touch-Friendly Navigation: Those tiny hyperlinks which are clean to click with a mouse can be frustratingly fiddly on a touchscreen. Make remarkable your buttons and hyperlinks are large enough to tap without troubles with a finger.

3.

Optimized Images: We cited this inside the final economic ruin, but it's miles well worth repeating: massive snap shots can gradual down your net net page. And on mobile, pace is even more crucial. So, optimize those pix!

4.

Viewport Meta Tag: This little piece of HTML code tells browsers to adjust the width and scaling of your page to healthy the display. If your website lacks this, it can reason a frustrating enjoy for cellular customers.

5.

Avoid Flash: Many mobile browsers don't assist Flash, so it's far brilliant to avoid it for critical factors of your website on-line.

6.

Testing: Last however no longer least, check your internet site on-line on wonderful gadgets and display display screen sizes to make sure it's miles virtually mobile-fine. Google's Mobile-Friendly Test tool may be an tremendous starting point!

And there you have got it – the quality information of cell-quality layout! Remember, in cutting-edge on-the-skip global, a mobile-exceptional internet web page isn't just awesome to have – it's far a should. So, skip forth and make your net website an area in which each visitor feels at domestic, regardless of what tool they will be using. Catch you inside the next bankruptcy!

Let's test yourself!

1. What does URL stand for?

a) Underlying Resource Locator

b) Uniform Resource Locator

c) Universal Retrieval Link

d) Unique Resource Link

2. What's the cause of Meta Tags in search engine advertising and marketing?

a) To help beautify the internet web page

b) To assist search engines like google apprehend the content material material of a website

c) To help growth the loading velocity of a internet web page

d) To make the net website online look greater colorful

three. When optimizing content material cloth, wherein have to your key-word ideally appear?

a) Only within the conclusion

b) Just as soon as in the middle of the content

c) In the number one a hundred-a hundred and fifty terms, and absolutely at a few level inside the content fabric

d) As typically as feasible, despite the fact that it sounds unnatural

4. What is an prolonged-tail key-phrase?

a) A key-phrase this is longer than 10 characters

b) A key-word with a tail icon subsequent to it

c) A specific key-word phrase that usually consists of 3 or greater terms

d) A key-word related to animal tails

five. Why should we optimize snap shots on our internet site?

a) To make the net web site extra colourful

## Chapter 5: What Is Link Building?

Link building is the system of obtaining links from specific net websites that issue decrease lower back on your internet website online. Think of these hyperlinks as votes of self perception, telling search engines like google and yahoo that your content material is valuable and really really worth sharing. The extra terrific, applicable links you have, the more likely serps like google are to view your internet website as an expert for your location of interest. This, in flip, can lead to better rankings and additional site site visitors.

Why is Link Building Important?

Google and precise search engines like google like google and yahoo like google use hyperlinks as a key factor in their rating algorithms. In essence, they cope with links like guidelines. If masses of valid websites link for your content material cloth, it want to be correct, proper? By constructing a sturdy hyperlink profile, you could beautify your internet website's credibility and are seeking engine scores.

Link Building Strategies: Making Friends the Right Way

1.

Create Amazing Content: It all begins offevolved proper here. If your content material is valuable, informative, or exciting, humans will genuinely need to link to it. Be the lifestyles of the seo party with impossible to resist content material material cloth that others cannot help but proportion.

2.

Reach Out to Industry Influencers: Don't be shy! Reach out to bloggers, reporters, and distinctive influencers on your niche. Share your content material material with them and ask in the event that they had be willing to hyperlink to it in the event that they locate it treasured. Remember, flattery can skip an prolonged way – truly be real and well mannered.

three.

Guest Posting: Offer to write down a vacationer positioned up for a few other net website on your area of hobby. This may be a win-win scenario: the host internet web page gets unfastened content fabric, and also you get a precious one manner hyperlink. Just make certain the net site you are writing for is relevant and professional.

4.

Build Relationships: Networking is high inside the international of link building. Join on-line groups, boards, and social media businesses associated with your niche. Participate in discussions, percentage your understanding, and help others. As you construct relationships, people can be much more likely to hyperlink in your content material.

5.

Broken Link Building: Find damaged hyperlinks on brilliant internet web sites and propose your personal relevant content material fabric as a opportunity. This may be a tremendous manner to benefit a one-manner hyperlink on the same time as also helping the internet site proprietor repair their damaged hyperlinks. Win-win!

6.

Testimonials and Reviews: Offer to put in writing a testimonial or evaluate for a services or products you have got were given used, and ask inside the event that that they had be inclined to link again for your website in return.

A Word of Caution: Avoiding Bad Link Building Habits

Not all link building techniques are created same. Beware of spammy strategies or purchasing low-first-rate oneway hyperlinks, as the ones can damage your website on-line's rankings in the end. Stick to moral, white-hat link building practices to ensure lasting fulfillment.

And there you have it – your introduction to the appropriate global of hyperlink building! As you embark on your off-web page search engine optimization adventure, bear in mind that it's far all approximately building relationships and developing charge for others. So, flow forth and make friends – your net internet website online's authority and rankings will thanks!

## 5.2. Social Media and are looking for engine advertising

Today, we are going to take a interesting journey into the bustling universe of social media and its powerful connection with seek engine marketing. Yes, you heard it proper! This financial destroy is all approximately how Facebook, Twitter, Instagram, and unique social systems can turn out to be a workout-changer for your search engine advertising method.

Ready to unlock the potential of social media for seo? Buckle up, and allow's roll!

The Unseen Bond among Social Media and search engine advertising

While social media indicators do no longer immediately impact your are searching for engine ratings, social media and search engine marketing are interwoven in tactics which is probably difficult to disregard. Imagine social media as your net internet page's extroverted fine buddy at the celebration, introducing your content material fabric to functionality fans throughout the globe.

Greater visibility method better traffic, and prolonged visitors brings a better hazard of inbound hyperlinks and shares, all of which sends high best signals to engines like google like google about your net website.

Dance Steps to Synchronize Social Media with search engine optimization

1.

Sharing is Caring: The first step in your social media and seo dance is to percentage your content material on your social systems. Every percentage is an invite on your target audience to visit your website, find out your content fabric, and probably hyperlink again to it from their non-public structures.

2.

Engage Like There's No Tomorrow: Social media isn't always a one-manner street; it is an interactive playground. Engage collectively with your target audience with the useful resource of responding to comments, taking part in discussions, and fostering a experience of community. This not exceptional enhances your emblem's photo however additionally drives greater internet web page visitors in your internet web page.

3.

Social Media for Link Building: We all understand how essential back hyperlinks are inside the search engine advertising and marketing worldwide (recall our previous monetary break?). Social media offers a powerful platform for networking with influencers, sharing your content cloth material, and earning the ones valuable oneway links.

4.

Boost Your Content with Social Media Ads: Got a few advertising rate variety to spare? Try boosting your posts using social media marketing and advertising. This can put your content fabric fabric inside the front of a larger, more centered target audience, developing your acquire and capability for net internet site traffic.

five.

Optimize Your Social Media Profiles: Your social media profile is your virtual storefront. Make pleasant to optimize it with the useful resource of which includes applicable key phrases for your bio or about segment, and, of path, usually link over again on your internet web site.

6.

Use Hashtags Wisely: Hashtags are not just modern day; they'll be beneficial. They help categorize your content material, making it an awful lot less complex for social media clients to locate. Just remember to use them sparingly and make certain they will be relevant to your content material fabric.

7.

Leverage User-Generated Content: Encourage your fanatics to percent their very very very own content material associated with your brand or products. User-generated content material cloth now not most effective engages your goal marketplace however additionally offers you extra content fabric to percentage and may boom your emblem's visibility.

The Life of the Social Media Party: Fresh and Engaging Content

In the world of social media, content fabric fabric is king, queen, and the entire court docket docket. Regularly sharing clean, attractive content material is the important thing to preserving an lively social media presence. But do not pressure if you do now not have time to create new content material each day.

You can use ChatGPT, repurpose older content cloth, proportion relevant content fabric from others, or create new posts highlighting precise elements of your current content material cloth.

And it in reality is the extended tour of our Social Media and are trying to find engine advertising exploration! Just recall, in the ever-evolving worldwide of digital advertising, seo and social media are two peas in a pod. They may not constantly immediately engage, but when they artwork together, they might help your online presence jump.

five.Three. Content Marketing

Hello, destiny seek engine marketing authorities! It's time to reveal the net web page to a brand new financial disaster in our interesting seo adventure. This time, we're moving into the colorful international of content material fabric material advertising and discovering the manner it weaves into the broader tapestry of are looking for engine advertising.

Buckle up, because we're about to expose how first-class content can be the superpower that propels your internet web page to the top of are looking for engine effects. Are you geared up to become a content material advertising maestro? Let's dive proper in!

Content Marketing and seek engine marketing and advertising: An Unbreakable Bond

Content advertising and marketing and seo are like aspects of the same coin. While are seeking engine advertising and marketing focuses on making your internet internet page attractive to search engines like google and yahoo, content material cloth advertising and advertising and marketing is all about appealing to human readers.

You see, search engines like google like google aim to deliver the maximum relevant and excellent content material cloth fabric to clients, so by means of way of making terrific content material material, you are assisting search engines do their hobby!

# Chapter 6: The Content Marketing Symphony

Creating wonderful content material fabric isn't just about writing properly; it consists of a symphony of factors that come together to shape a fascinating narrative. Let's find out what it takes to compose a masterpiece in content advertising and advertising and marketing:

1.

Understanding Your Audience: Before you can create content fabric material that resonates, you need to realize who you're speaking to. Understand your target audience's interests, wishes, and worrying conditions. This will assist you create content material material cloth that now not great engages but additionally presents fee.

2.

Keyword Research: Just like in search engine optimization, keywords play a starring feature in content material material advertising and marketing. Use equipment like Google Keyword Planner or Ahrefs to find out relevant key terms that your target audience is attempting to find, and weave the ones into your content material absolutely.

3.

Creating Valuable Content: This is the coronary coronary heart and soul of content material cloth marketing and advertising. From weblog posts and articles to motion pictures and infographics, your content material fabric cloth ought to be designed to offer fee, answer questions, clear up issues, or entertain. Remember, brilliant over quantity is the golden rule!

4.

search engine advertising and marketing and advertising Optimization: Once you've got were given crafted your splendid content cloth, recollect to optimize it for search engines like google and yahoo like google. Include your keywords certainly, use meta tags, and shape your content material fabric for clarity. Think decrease lower back to our in advance chapters to refresh your reminiscence on those essential elements!

5.

Promotion: Writing wonderful content cloth is simplest 1/2 of the war; you furthermore mght want to promote it. Share your content fabric on social media, ship it to your email list, and do not shrink back from achieving out to influencers to your vicinity of hobby who might be interested in sharing your content too.

6.

Regular Updates: The digital worldwide actions at warp tempo, and what have end up relevant the day before today might not be nowadays. Regularly examine and update your content material cloth material to ensure it remains valuable, correct, and seek engine marketing-excellent.

7.

Analyzing Performance: Just like numerous advertising and advertising approach, it's essential to degree the overall basic overall performance of your content material fabric advertising and marketing efforts. Use gear like Google Analytics to appearance what is walking and in which there may be room for improvement.

The Power of Storytelling in Content Marketing

In content fabric advertising and advertising and marketing and marketing, storytelling is your thriller weapon. Stories have a unique power to interact readers, making your content material cloth more memorable and shareable. Whether you are sharing a case test, providing data, or explaining a complex state of affairs depend, try to weave a tale that your goal marketplace can connect with.

And that concludes our deep-dive into content advertising and marketing and marketing! Remember, with reference to winning at seo, compelling, first rate content material material is your maximum effective best friend.

So get available, begin growing, and permit your content material fabric do the speaking. Keep a be careful for our subsequent financial disaster, wherein we will preserve unlocking the secrets and techniques and techniques of searching for engine advertising and marketing. Until then, glad writing!

Let's check yourself!

1. If seek engine advertising and Content Marketing had been at a zoo, which of the following excellent describes their relationship?

a. They're like lions and gazelles – continuously at odds.

b. They're like squirrels and wooden – one is constantly chasing the opposite.

c. They're like dolphins and water – you can't virtually have one without the possibility.

d. They're like penguins in the barren area – they do not belong collectively.

2. Why have to you take into account social media as your internet web site's extroverted extremely good buddy on the party?

a. Because social media continuously brings the awesome snacks.

b. Because social media introduces your content material cloth to ability fanatics in the course of the globe, driving site traffic for your internet web site.

c. Because social media systems make notable DJs.

d. Because social media in no manner forgets your birthday.

three. What sort of hyperlinks are taken into consideration the 'white chocolate' of the search engine advertising worldwide because of their significance and desirability?

a. Chain hyperlinks

b. Sausage links

c. Backlinks

d. Missing hyperlinks

4. If content material fabric is king inside the international of Content Marketing, what is probably taken into consideration the queen?

a. Keyword stuffing

b. The contemporary meme

c. Value to the reader

d. Funny cat movement photos

five. In the symphony of Content Marketing, what feature does understanding your purpose market play?

a. It's the conductor, guiding the entire usual normal overall performance.

b. It's the triangle participant, only applicable occasionally.

c. It's the charge ticket booth, figuring out what number of human beings show up.

d. It's the janitor, cleaning up after the general performance.

6. Local search engine optimization

6.1. Local seek engine marketing

Putting Your Business on the Map!

Hello, searching for engine marketing and advertising and marketing fans! We're once more on the journey of discovery, and in recent times we're speaking approximately a few element a piece more… community. We're going to discover the bustling neighborhood of Local SEO! Grab your virtual maps and allow's navigate the streets of this critical element of seo.

Local are searching for engine marketing: Your Friendly Neighborhood Spider-Man of are seeking for engine advertising

So, what is Local search engine optimization? Imagine are searching for engine advertising and marketing as a superhero. If seek engine advertising is Superman, flying round assisting each person worldwide, then Local SEO is greater like your high-quality community Spider-Man, focusing its superpowers on a selected locality – your business organisation's network!

Local are seeking engine advertising is all approximately promoting your services and products to nearby clients at the appropriate time they are looking for them. It enables your commercial company seem in neighborhood are seeking for consequences on search engines like google like google. Think about whilst you look for 'coffee save near me'. The close by espresso stores that pop up first? That's Local search engine optimization working its magic!

Why Local seo Matters

Now, you is probably questioning: "Why need to I care approximately Local seo?" The answer is straightforward – because of the truth your customers do! A big portion of all Google searches are for local facts.

Many clients, who search for nearby organizations on cellular gadgets, call or go to those groups rapidly after their are looking for.

Local search engine optimization could make your business more seen in neighborhood seek results, electricity extra web site traffic for your internet site, and in the long run result in greater clients – and who does now not need more clients?

The Key Components of Local are trying to find engine advertising

Local search engine optimization may seem like a huge metropolis to navigate, but do not worry – we've got were given had been given have been given your decrease again! Here are some key landmarks that will help you recognize the close by search engine optimization panorama:

1.

Google My Business: This is your property base inside the worldwide of Local search engine marketing. It's a free tool from Google that helps you to manage how your company appears in Google Search and Maps. It's like your agency's very private little superhero lair!

2.

Online Reviews: These are just like the residents your superhero industrial organisation is defensive. Positive critiques can help boom your organization's visibility and increase the risk that a ability purchaser will go to your vicinity.

3.

Local Keywords: These are your superpowers. Including region-primarily based key phrases in your internet website content fabric can help beautify your visibility in nearby are searching for effects.

So, there you have got had been given it – a friendly creation to the sector of Local SEO! It's a powerful tool to have for your seek engine marketing software belt, specifically for small companies trying to make a massive effect. Stay tuned for our subsequent economic disaster, in which we're able to cross deeper into the interesting worldwide of seo. Until then, satisfied optimizing!

## 6.2 Optimizing Google My Business

Hello once more! So, we have set up that Local SEO is like your friendly network superhero. Now, allow's talk approximately your very very private superhero headquarters – Google My Business (GMB). It's time to roll up our virtual sleeves and get into the nitty-gritty of optimizing your GMB list.

Ready? Let's dive right in!

Google My Business: Your Local search engine optimization Command Center

Think of your Google My Business list as your business's virtual storefront. When humans look for your commercial company, it's far regularly the number one issue they see. It's like your commercial commercial enterprise organisation's virtual ID card, displaying key data like your employer name, address, hours, opinions, and extra.

But a GMB listing is greater than really a web directory. It's an interactive platform that could assist boom your community search engine advertising and marketing and marketing, lure greater customers, or maybe allow you to engage together together with your target market right away. Cool, right?

Optimizing Your GMB Listing: The Friendly Guide

Optimizing your Google My Business listing is like redecorating your superhero headquarters. You want to make sure it is realistic, informative, and represents your business agency because it need to be. Here's how you can do it:

1.    Complete Your Profile: Just like how a superhero needs their in form, your GMB list needs whole records. Fill out every segment – commercial company name, cope with, phone

amount, internet website online, hours, lessons, and further. The more information you offer, the tons less tough it's miles for customers to find and hook up with you.

2. Be Consistent: Make wonderful the statistics on your GMB listing fits the statistics to your internet web page and special online directories. Consistency is fundamental inside the international of Local search engine optimization.

three. Add High-Quality Photos: A photograph is well sincerely worth 1000 terms, and this is surely real for your GMB listing. High-first-class snap shots of your commercial enterprise enterprise, merchandise, or services have to make your listing extra attractive and attractive to potential customers.

four. Collect and Respond to Reviews: Encourage your clients to depart critiques for your GMB list. Not only do opinions improve your local search engine optimization, but further they collect accept as true with with capability clients. Remember to reply to evaluations too – it is a great manner to show you fee client comments.

five.    Use Google Posts: Google Posts are like mini-commercials or social media posts that show up to your GMB listing. They're a outstanding manner to percentage updates, promotions, sports, or information with people who discover your business enterprise on Google.

6.    Analyze Insights: Google offers treasured insights on how customers find your listing, what actions they take, and extra. Use this statistics to apprehend your target market better and to make upgrades on your list.

And there you have got had been given it, pals – a pleasant guide to optimizing your Google My Business list. Remember, just like any superhero, your GMB listing is high-quality as real due to the truth the attempt you positioned into it. So, take the time to optimize it and watch because it allows increase your nearby search engine marketing efforts!

6.Three. Local Keywords

Hey there! Are you geared up to discover each other mystery weapon in your Local search engine optimization arsenal? Today, we are getting up close and private with Local Keywords. Consider them your mystery sauce, the magic phrases which can help your internet site pop up in community searches. Ready to sprinkle a number of this magic onto your net website? Let's dive in!

# Chapter 7: Your Secret Handshake With Search Engines

First subjects first, what are community key terms? Well, they'll be quite just like the keywords we've got were given were given already noted, but with a community twist. They embody unique locations on the side of your aim key terms. For example, in case you're a pizza location in Brooklyn, your nearby key-phrase might be "top notch pizza in Brooklyn".

Using close by key phrases on your content material is sort of a thriller handshake with search engines like google like google and yahoo. It tells them, "Hey, my commercial enterprise is right right here on this location!" This permits search engines like google suit your internet site with close by are trying to find queries, bringing greater focused web page site visitors your way.

Why Local Keywords are the Bees' Knees

Now, you may wonder why you need to fuss approximately neighborhood keywords. Well, here's a fun truth: nearly half of of all Google searches are for community facts. And guess what? If your content fabric is peppered with applicable close by key phrases, your business enterprise is much more likely to show up in these searches. Sweet, right?

But the perks do now not prevent there! Local key terms moreover help you appeal to awesome traffic. That's due to the fact people using community seek phrases are often prepared to achieve this. So, if your content pops up even as someone searches for "canine groomer in San Francisco", there can be an exquisite chance they're in need of your offerings right now!

Finding and Using Local Keywords: A Friendly Guide

Finding the right nearby keywords is not a recreation of conceal-and-are looking for. It's more of a treasure hunt! And like every proper treasure hunt, you want the right tools and strategies. Here's a pleasant manual to help you out:

1.

Think Like a Local: Start through setting your self in your customer's footwear. What phrases need to they use to look for your services for your place? Don't forget to don't forget community slang and colloquialisms!

2.

Use Keyword Research Tools: Tools like Google's Keyword Planner or Moz's Keyword Explorer can help you discover famous neighborhood key phrases related to your agency.

three.

Check Out the Competition: Look at what close by keywords your competition are using. You might probably find out a few keyword goldmines!

four.

Implement Your Keywords: Once you've got your neighborhood key terms, sprinkle them in the end of your website — to your titles, meta descriptions, headers, content material, or even URLs. But bear in thoughts, use them obviously. Keyword stuffing is a massive no-no!

5.

Monitor and Adjust: searching for engine advertising is a marathon, no longer a sprint. Keep a watch regular in your analytics to peer how your community key phrases are performing and modify as important.

With those magic phrases, you can assist guide nearby clients right to your digital doorstep. Stay tuned for extra thrilling seo adventures in our subsequent bankruptcy! Until then, glad optimizing!

Let's test your self!

1. If Local are trying to find engine advertising were a superhero, which of these might be its superpower?

a) Flying spherical the world in seconds

b) Turning invisible

c) Helping your industrial employer seem in nearby search results

d) Time tour

2. Your Google My Business listing is like:

a) A dusty antique cellular phone ebook

b) A dull industrial corporation meeting

c) Your business business enterprise's virtual ID card

d) A bowl of broccoli

three. What's one manner to optimize your Google My Business list?

a) Fill it with as many buzzwords as possible

b) Only encompass the naked minimal information

c) Fill out each phase with correct and consistent information

d) Ignore it and desire for the pleasant

4. What's a neighborhood key-word?

a) A shape of special bird

b) A key that opens all doorways in your metropolis

c) A key-word collectively with your area added to it

d) A thriller code to enter a close-by membership

five. How can you operate local key phrases to enhance your community seo?

a) By stuffing as many as possible into your content material

b) By ignoring them simply

c) By sprinkling them without a doubt at some point of your net website

d) By writing them in invisible ink

Hey, preserve in thoughts to test your solutions on the give up of the e-book!

7. Technical seek engine marketing

7.1. Page Load Speed

are trying to find engine advertising and advertising virtuosos! Ever heard of the pronouncing, "sluggish and regular wins the race"? Well, as an entire lot as we adore an extraordinary tortoise-and-the-hare myth, it is not quite how things artwork in the land of seo. When it comes on your website's load pace, being a Speedy Gonzales is the call of the sport.

So, buckle up and permit's zoom into the arena of Page Load Speed!

The Need for Speed in search engine advertising-Land

Page Load Speed, in clean phrases, is how short your net web site loads whilst someone clicks on your web internet site. And wager what? Both your human traffic and the hunt engine bots have a want for tempo.

Here's why: humans are busy. They need to find what they are looking for quick and effortlessly. If your web page takes too prolonged to load, they may be probably to hit the decrease again button faster than you may say 'search engine optimization'. In fact, research show that a put off of in reality one second in net page reaction can bring about a 7% discount in conversions. Yikes!

And it's no longer just your site visitors who understand a short internet page. Search engines do, too. Google, as an instance, considers net web page load velocity as one of its rating factors. A faster website can purpose better visibility in seek effects. That's a win-win!

Tools to Check and Improve Page Speed

Now, you might be wondering, "How do I understand if my website is a pace demon or a sluggish poke?" That's in which device are available handy. There are several outstanding unfastened tools to be had that not handiest measure your net site's speed however moreover provide you with insights on a manner to decorate it.

Google's PageSpeed Insights is one such tool. It rankings your net web page on a scale of 0 to a hundred and offers pointers for improvement. Another tool is GTMetrix, which gives an entire have a look at your internet web page's tempo commonplace overall overall performance. Pingdom is another famous desire that offers smooth-to-recognize opinions.

Turbocharging Your Page Load Speed

So, how do you bypass approximately dashing up your internet web page? Here are a few best suggestions:

1.

Optimize Your Images: Big, cumbersome pix can gradual down your web site. Use tool to compress your images without losing first-rate, and endure in thoughts the usage of a format like JPEG 2000, JPEG XR, or WebP that offers superior compression.

2.

Minify CSS, JavaScript, and HTML: By optimizing your code (which encompass removing areas, commas, and other useless characters), you can boom your net web page speed.

three.

Reduce Redirects: Each time a page redirects to another internet web page, your visitor faces more time looking earlier to the HTTP request-reaction cycle to complete.

four.

Leverage Browser Caching: Browsers cache an entire lot of facts (like stylesheets, pictures, JavaScript documents, and so forth.) so that after a visitor comes again in your internet page, the browser would now not want to reload the whole internet web page.

five.

Use a Content Distribution Network (CDN): CDNs are networks of servers which may be used to distribute the weight of handing over content cloth cloth. Essentially, copies of your internet page are stored at a couple of, geographically numerous records centers so customers have quicker and additional reliable get admission to in your internet site on line.

Remember, the need for pace isn't quite a whole lot maintaining the search engine bots satisfied. It's about developing a better, smoother enjoy for your clients. And a glad man or woman is much more likely to end up a dedicated customer. So, put on your tempo goggles, stir up your engines, and permit's make your internet site the Speedy Gonzales of the search engine optimization-land!

## 7.2. Clean Code

Ready to roll up your sleeves and get your arms a piece dirty? Don't worry, we're not speakme about gardening. Today, we're diving deep into the coronary heart of your net site – the code. It's time to take a look at the art of tidying up... Our code, that is! Let's dive in.

## Clean Code, Happy Website

In the area of programming, 'easy code' is code that is simple to understand, smooth to check, and easy to keep. It's code it is written in a way it honestly is constant, logical, and green. Clean code is like a properly-prepared closet – the whole lot has its region, and there is no unnecessary clutter.

Why does this rely for seek engine advertising and marketing? Well, search engine bots are like fast little librarians. They 'take a look at' your internet web web page's code to understand what your internet net page is about and in which to rank it in are trying to find consequences.

If your code is straightforward and well-organized, those bots can zip thru it speedy and without issue. But if your code is messy and cluttered, it may gradual down these bots or maybe confuse them. And a careworn bot isn't a satisfied bot.

## Tidying Up Your Code

So, how do you tidy up your code? Here are a few best suggestions:

1.

Minify Your Code: Minifying your code approach removing needless characters (like regions and line breaks) and simplifying it as a whole lot as possible without converting its functionality. It's like decluttering your closet – you're eliminating a few trouble you do now not want.

2.

Use Semantic HTML: This way the use of HTML tags in a way that represents the content material material contained in them. For instance, the usage of <header>, <footer>, and <article> tags for your header, footer, and article content material material, respectively. This lets in searching for engine bots recognize your content material cloth higher.

three.

Remove Duplicate Code: If you have the equal chew of code in more than one locations, it is time to consolidate. Having reproduction code is like having identical black shirts in your closet – one is sufficient!

4.

Keep Your CSS External: This manner storing your CSS code in an out of doors document and linking to it out of your HTML. This makes your HTML document cleanser and simpler to read.

Tools for Cleaning Up

Thankfully, you do no longer need to tidy up your code via way of hand. There are several gear available that can help. For minifying your code, strive equipment like UglifyJS (for JavaScript) or CSSNano (for CSS). For finding and removing reproduction code, attempt gear like JSCPD or CSSLint.

# Chapter 8: Fundamentals Of Search Engines

As we delve deeper into the multifaceted realm of Search Engine Optimization (search engine marketing), it's far crucial to take a step returned and understands the very platform that seo is designed to optimize for: serps. These effective, difficult systems function the gateways to the boundless information to be had on the Internet, shaping patron opinions and influencing the way companies and people have interaction on-line. Understanding the fundamentals of engines like google like google and yahoo is not truely a theoretical exercise however a practical necessity for actually all of us important approximately studying search engine marketing.

This section, "Fundamentals of Search Engines," serves as a foundational framework to apprehend the internal workings of search engines like google like google and yahoo. We will solve the complicated algorithms and information systems that permit serps like google to locate, rank, and show net pages primarily based mostly on a person's query. This expertise will empower you to formulate seo strategies which is probably aligned with how search engines like google like google perform, extensively growing the efficacy of your optimization efforts.

We'll start by way of the use of way of discussing how engines like google like google artwork, exploring the steps of crawling, indexing, and ranking that collectively make a contribution to the Search Engine Results Pages (SERPs) anybody have interaction with each day. Subsequently, we're capable of delve into the important detail principles and terminology which might be crucial to know-how serps—phrases like "PageRank," "bots," "spiders," and "are searching for for signals," amongst others.

As we progress, we're able to have a take a look at the location of are seeking for engine advertising inside the broader context of virtual advertising and why know-how the mechanics of engines like google like google is critical for an powerful digital marketing approach. Finally, we are able to address ethical problems, delving into what practices are considered moral or "white-hat," and what falls under the "black-hat" beauty, permitting you to make knowledgeable selections that could stand the test of time in a continuously evolving virtual landscape.

Understanding the fundamentals of search engines will no longer best enlighten you approximately the underlying mechanisms that have an effect on SERPs but also assist you appreciate the intricacies of search engine optimization. It serves as a cornerstone upon which to gather greater superior expertise in key-phrase studies, on-net page optimization, technical search engine optimization, and first-rate areas that make up the complex mosaic of seek engine advertising expertise.

So, whether or no longer you're an entrepreneur aiming to elevate your employer, a virtual marketer in search of to sharpen your skills, or an enthusiast keen to apprehend the virtual international better, this section guarantees to provide precious insights that can function building blocks to your seo adventure. Sit returned, soak up, and permit's demystify the algorithms and operations that strength the search engines like google like google and yahoo we rely on every day.

## 2.1. How Search Engines Work

Understanding how serps paintings is much like unlocking a thriller this is full-size to the current virtual experience. Every day, billions of searches are completed on systems like Google, Bing, and Yahoo, supporting customers discover information, corporations, merchandise, and services. At the coronary heart of this interplay lies a complicated tool of algorithms, information structures, and generation that make the ones right now connections among customers and data viable. In this segment, we can delve into the mechanisms that permit search engines like google and yahoo to move slowly, index, and rank internet web sites, thereby growing the Search Engine Results Pages (SERPs) that we see while we type in a question.

The Lifecycle of a Search Query: An Overview

At a immoderate diploma, the functioning of a are looking for engine can be broken down into 3 most important levels:

1.      Crawling: This is the approach wherein attempting to find engine bots, moreover referred to as crawlers or spiders, scour the internet to discover new or updated pages.

2.      Indexing: Once the pages are observed, they're listed and stored in massive databases from wherein they will be retrieved on the identical time as applicable to a are trying to find query.

3.      Ranking: When a person inputs a are in search of question, the search engine's set of guidelines assesses the listed pages and ranks them based totally mostly on various factors,

presenting the maximum relevant and authoritative consequences to the customer.

Let's discover every of those tiers in detail.

Crawling: The Digital Cartographers

The internet is an ever-developing universe of pages, and are searching for engine crawlers act as virtual cartographers, mapping out this complicated terrain. These crawlers observe hyperlinks from noted net pages to new pages, recording their findings and sending them decrease back to be saved in the seek engine's database. The frequency of crawling can range based totally mostly on numerous factors, which include the internet web page's significance, frequency of content fabric material updates, and technical elements like internet site velocity and sitemaps.

Various types of bots carry out specialized skills. For instance, Googlebot is Google's internet crawling bot, whilst Bingbot serves the equal cause for Bing. These bots depend upon a series of algorithms to determine which websites to transport slowly, how frequently, and how many pages to fetch from every net website.

Indexing: The Digital Library

Indexing is the subsequent step within the are trying to find engine's lifecycle. Once an internet page is decided, the crawler methods and stores the statistics in a manner that makes it retrievable for the duration of a person search. This is similar to cataloging a e-book in a library. The search engine creates an index based on textual content content fabric material, pics, motion pictures, and one-of-a-kind media documents on the internet net page. Metadata like keywords, headings, and hyperlinks are also considered within the path of indexing.

While indexing, search engines like google and yahoo like google moreover observe severa factors just like the first-rate of content material fabric, meta-descriptions, and the relevance of inbound links pointing to the net net web page. Factors like canonical tags and robots.Txt documents can also have an impact on what gets listed.

Ranking: The Algorithmic Symphony

The 1/3 and maximum essential degree is ranking. Once a client enters a question, the quest engine's algorithms get to paintings, pulling relevant records from the index and imparting it in the shape of SERPs. A multitude of things impacts the ranking of these outcomes. Google, for example, considers over hundred factors while rating net pages, despite the fact that no longer all are given equal weight. Some of those elements encompass:

1.	Relevance: How nicely the content cloth fits the query.

2.	Authority: The range and awesome of hyperlinks pointing to the web page.

three. Usability: Site velocity, cellular-friendliness, and person enjoy.

4.      Content Quality: Originality, depth, and shape of the content material cloth.

five.    Personalization: User data, location, and settings.

The unique algorithms for score are cautiously guarded change secrets and strategies and strategies and are continuously evolving, however know-how those primary requirements can circulate an prolonged way in learning search engine optimization.

Search Algorithms: The Evolving Paradigms

Search engines regularly update their algorithms to enhance search accuracy and consumer experience. Google, for instance, often tweaks its set of policies and every so often releases massive updates which could drastically effect SERPs. Some landmark set of guidelines updates encompass Google Panda, which penalizes low-nice net sites; Google Penguin, focused on lowering the effectiveness of black-hat seek engine advertising techniques; and Google

Hummingbird, which considers the context and semantics of trying to find queries. Understanding those updates is vital for seo practitioners who want to comply their strategies to live earlier of the game.

Structured Data and Rich Snippets

Search engines are increasingly more incorporating installed statistics and rich snippets into their algorithms. Structured records permits search engines like google and yahoo like google like google to better apprehend the content cloth cloth and context of internet pages, enhancing the amazing and relevance of search effects. Rich snippets, alternatively, present statistics from the net web page right now at the SERP, enhancing person revel in.

Mobile Search and Voice Search

With the proliferation of smartphones and voice-activated devices, cellular and voice are searching for for have grow to be tremendous issues for search engines. Mobile-first indexing approach that Google predominantly makes use of the cell version of a internet internet site for ranking and indexing. Voice seek algorithms also undergo in thoughts factors like herbal language processing and question-based totally truely queries.

Ethical Considerations: White Hat vs. Black Hat

While search engines like google reason to offer the most applicable and outstanding effects, a few try to game the machine the usage of unethical or "black-hat" techniques like key-phrase stuffing, cloaking, and hyperlink farming. Search engines constantly update their algorithms to penalize such practices. Ethical or "white-hat" search engine optimization makes a speciality of developing charge for clients via adhering to appearance engine pointers.

## 2.2. Key Search Engine Concepts and Terminology

Navigating the world of seo (are seeking engine advertising) can regularly enjoy like venturing proper into a labyrinth packed with jargon, acronyms, and concepts that seem overseas to the uninitiated. However, like any region, facts the specific terminology and key concepts is a crucial step towards reading search engine advertising. This section dreams to demystify those phrases, exploring the vital thoughts that form the backbone of ways serps feature and interact with internet websites. Whether you are an search engine advertising newcomer, a commercial organization proprietor looking for to decorate your online presence, or perhaps a pro virtual marketer attempting to find to refresh your records, this guide is designed to enlighten you.

Search Query

At the coronary coronary coronary heart of every interaction with a are searching for engine is the "search query," often called "key terms" or "looking for phrases." This is the phrase or query that someone sorts into the search subject. Search queries can variety from single phrases like "weather" to complicated sentences like "a way to bake a chocolate cake from scratch." Understanding the nuances of are seeking for queries, which includes their cause, period, and specificity, is pivotal for effective are seeking engine advertising.

SERP (Search Engine Results Page)

SERP is the acronym for Search Engine Results Page, the net page that displays the results for a given seek query. It usually consists of each herbal and paid listings, on the side of severa different elements like featured snippets, knowledge graphs, and neighborhood maps, counting on the are trying to find question.

Organic vs. Paid Results

Organic Results: These are listings that seem clearly in SERPs based totally at the seek engine's set of guidelines. Organic consequences are taken into consideration more credible and collect the majority of clicks.

Paid Results: Also called Pay-Per-Click (PPC) outcomes, those are advertisements that groups pay for to seem on SERPs. They are commonly categorized as "Ad" or "Sponsored" and seem at the pinnacle or backside of the net internet web page.

Crawlers, Spiders, and Bots

These are computerized software program program marketers that scour the internet to discover, index, and replace net pages in a are seeking engine's database. Different search engines have their own crawlers; as an instance, Google's is known as Googlebot, and Bing's is called Bingbot. Understanding the way to facilitate effective crawling thru techniques like sitemap submissions can drastically effect your net website's searching for engine advertising overall performance.

Indexing

Indexing is the manner of storing internet pages in a search engine's database after they had been determined by using way of crawlers. The are seeking engine's index acts as a large digital library, storing billions of net pages that may be speedy retrieved at the equal time as applicable to a are seeking query. Technical factors like robots.Txt and meta tags can manipulate what additives of your internet web page get indexed.

Algorithms

Algorithms are units of tips and calculations that search engines like google use to determine the ranking of net pages for each are searching for query. Search engines like Google use complex and intently guarded algorithms, up to date often, to make sure applicable and superb outcomes.

## Chapter 9: Keyword Research And Analysis

The international of Search Engine Optimization (search engine advertising and advertising and marketing) can often enjoy like a labyrinth, teeming with technicalities and nuanced practices which can make or spoil your digital presence. However, if there is one cornerstone that holds the entire shape of search engine advertising and marketing and advertising collectively, it's far key-word studies and evaluation. This bankruptcy objectives to feature an important guide to the multi-faceted worldwide of key terms, the atomic devices of search engine optimization, dropping moderate on why they will be important, the way to move approximately studying them, and the manner to harness their energy on your benefit.

Keywords are the bridge that be part of customers' queries to relevant content cloth. When someone makes use of a are trying to find engine, they will be essentially posing a question or mentioning a need, albeit frequently in a very abbreviated shape. The search engine's venture is to understand this want and provide the maximum relevant and precious solution. Keywords play a pivotal function on this speak between the character and the hunt engine. They act as symptoms, signposts, or even qualifiers that guide the search engine algorithms in information the context, relevance, and satisfactory of internet pages. Therefore, studying the art work and technological knowledge of key-word studies and evaluation isn't handiest a advocated seo tactic; it's miles a essential necessity.

But do not be wrong—key-word research isn't always just about locating the most searched phrases and stuffing them into your content fabric. It's a strategic exercise that desires a deep know-how of your target market, market tendencies, and competitive landscape. It calls for analytical prowess to interpret information, creative capabilities to end up aware about possibilities, and strategic wondering to integrate key terms seamlessly into various factors of your net internet site on-line—from content material cloth and meta tags to URLs and anchor texts.

This financial ruin will find out severa elements of key-word research and assessment, together with its significance in seek engine advertising and marketing, mounted research techniques, aggressive assessment, and the ever-evolving concept of semantic searching for and lengthy-tail key phrases. Whether you are a novice seeking to get a grip for your internet site's search engine optimization or a seasoned marketer aiming for the coveted first-net web page ranking, know-how the amazing statistics of key-word research and assessment will arm you with the system you need to succeed.

So, buckle up as we dive into this critical factor of SEO, laying a stable basis for practices which could pressure measurable effects, decorate consumer enjoy, and function you as an expert in your situation.

## 3.1. Importance of Keywords in search engine marketing

Search Engine Optimization (search engine optimization) is a multidimensional workout, a continuously evolving problem that adapts to technological enhancements and adjustments in consumer conduct. Among the severa factors that represent the complicated global of seo, keywords keep a position of brilliant importance. This financial smash desires to delve deeply into the importance of key phrases, analyzing why they may be critical, how they have got an effect on numerous search engine optimization factors, and why their position has quality received in importance with the development of algorithms and person behaviors.

Keywords: The Fundamental Units of Search

Before venturing into the nuances, it's important to recognize what key phrases are. Keywords are the terms or terms that customers kind into search engines like google like google and yahoo at the same time as searching out facts, services, or merchandise. They are the linchpins that keep the search approach together, facilitating the man or woman's journey from a question to the most applicable content material. For serps like google and yahoo, key terms feature vital signposts, directing their algorithms to transport slowly, index, and present internet pages that healthy the client's are seeking for reason.

The Role of Keywords in Various seo Elements

Content Optimization: Keywords are critical to growing content material cloth that each serps like google and yahoo and customers find valuable. Proper key-phrase placement and density inside the content material can notably beautify the net net page's possibilities of ranking better in searching for results. It's critical to examine that 'key-word stuffing' is an antique and penalized exercise; the point of interest is now on natural, contextual use of key phrases.

Meta Tags and Descriptions: The understand tag and meta description are critical HTML elements that want to consist of applicable key phrases. This now not great boosts are seeking engine advertising and marketing but moreover improves the press-via rate (CTR) from the hunt consequences internet page, as clients are much more likely to click on on on results that carefully healthy their queries.

URL Structure: Keywords in URLs can make contributions to a page's search engine optimization basic performance. URLs that incorporate relevant key terms are regularly more intuitive and character-satisfactory, making them tons less difficult to don't forget and percent.

Internal and External Linking: Keywords additionally play a function in anchor text, impacting each internal linking strategies and one way link building efforts. Anchor text that consists of applicable keywords can provide contextual clues to search engines approximately the associated content material, thereby influencing its rating.

4. On-Page search engine marketing Optimization

On-web page search engine optimization is an indispensable detail of the present day-day digital technique. As the announcing goes, "If Content is King, then On-Page search engine optimization is the Throne." It is the tactical basis upon which the most impactful content material is built. On-web page seek engine advertising pertains to all the variables that you may manage inner your internet web site: assume of factors like your HTML tags, your content fabric satisfactory, your content fabric shape, key-word placement, photo optimization, and greater. However, it's far now not honestly about appealing the quest engine algorithms; at its middle, on-web net page search engine optimization is prepared supplying a stellar man or woman revel in.

In the approaching sections, we will delve deep into the nitty-gritty of on-net internet page seek engine advertising and marketing. We will explore how the cautious association of HTML tags can enhance your are seeking engine visibility, why the form of your URLs topics, and the way a image can indeed be actually definitely really worth 1000 clicks if properly optimized. We will check out:

1. Search engine advertising and marketing and advertising-Friendly Content Creation: We'll observe a way to write exceptional content material that now not nice ranks nicely but moreover engages and converts.

2. HTML Tags and Structured Data: We'll demystify the sector of HTML, looking at factors like name tags, meta descriptions, and the manner based totally statistics can beautify your visibility.

three. URL Structure and Permalinks: We'll dissect the anatomy of a URL and understand how a properly-crafted one can be every purchaser-quality and are attempting to find engine-great.

four.  Image Optimization and Alt Text: We'll scrutinize the way to make certain that your pix aren't slowing down your web web site and how they may be able to make contributions for your are searching for engine advertising goals.

This bankruptcy pursuits to be a complete manual, offering you with actionable insights and examined strategies for boosting your on-page search engine optimization. You'll come to appearance that studying on-net web web page seek engine advertising and advertising is similar to studying a musical tool; it's miles all approximately great-tuning the data until the complete composition involves lifestyles. Whether you are a newbie who's new to the search engine optimization sport or a pro veteran looking to refresh your knowledge, this chapter offers valuable nuggets of facts that allow you to growth your on-web web page search engine optimization sport to a professional degree.

five. Technical seo

Welcome to the thrilling and particularly mysterious global of Technical seo. If you have navigated through the earlier chapters on the fundamentals of seo, key-phrase studies, and on-web web page optimization, you are now moving into a website that underpins the complete seo surroundings. Technical SEO, regularly perceived due to the fact the extra 'geeky' part of seo, is honestly a pivotal issue that ensures your net internet web site's compatibility with are searching for engine hints. It's the framework upon which your content and on-net internet web page optimizations either thrive or falter.

Imagine your internet net web page as a car. Your content material cloth is the outside and indoors format—what attracts humans and maintains them snug. On-net web page seo is corresponding to the ergonomics and accessibility abilities—making sure humans can with out troubles get what they need. However, Technical search engine optimization is the engine, the transmission, and the suspension. Without the ones, your car might not even begin, not to say win any races. Simply positioned, studying Technical search engine advertising and marketing ensures that looking for engine spiders do not sincerely visit your net website online online, however additionally apprehend it, number one to higher rankings and, consequently, greater organic site visitors.

In this section, we are able to delve deep into the middle additives of Technical search engine optimization, starting from net website on line form and XML sitemaps to factors like cell optimization and place speed. We'll check the nuances of robots.Txt documents, find out the importance of sturdy and reachable internet internet sites, and take a look at out the promising however complex territory of structured statistics and rich snippets. Moreover, you may additionally benefit insights into the moral problems that encompass Technical are searching for engine advertising, placing you on a route that respects every era and customers.

If you have got got ever perplexed why your fantastic content cloth isn't generating the traffic it deserves, or why your key-word-optimized pages aren't ranking as excessive as they need to be, the answers often lie within the technical health of your net website. Failing to address technical troubles can be likened to constructing a stunning house on a shaky basis. Sooner or later, problems will rise up, and they may reason a extraordinary loss in searching for visibility and client engagement.

By the cease of this phase, you need to be well-prepared to perform a technical search engine optimization audit, choose out troubles that might be retaining your net internet website back, and put in force solutions at the way to optimize your web website on-line for every search engines like google like google and clients. Whether you are a company owner looking to beautify your internet website on-line's basic performance, or an aspiring seek engine advertising expert, understanding the intricacies of Technical search engine optimization will offer you with the machine to set up and hold a robust and sustainable on line presence.

So, buckle up and put together to delve into the technical elements that would make or harm your are trying to find engine advertising and marketing efforts. This journey may also additionally moreover get technical, however it is a road that ends within the coronary coronary heart of powerful seek engine advertising and marketing and marketing method.

five.1. Website Architecture and Navigation

When it entails Technical seo, the shape and navigation of your internet internet web page feature the cornerstone. They are corresponding to the blueprint and foundation of a house— elements that determine the strength, stability, and functionality of the shape. If the structure is defective or the navigation perplexing, you run the danger of the use of away traffic or, worse, in no way getting found by means of the usage of search engines like google like google and yahoo inside the first area. In this segment, we are capable of deep-dive into the significance of net internet site shape and navigation, recognize the standards in the once more of them, and become aware of exquisite practices which could remodel your website into an seo powerhouse.

## 6. Off-Page seo and Link Building

Welcome to the captivating domain of Off-Page search engine optimization and Link Building, a realm that extends an extended way past the content material cloth, shape, and technicalities of your net internet web site. While on-net web page and technical search engine optimization makes a speciality of optimizing your very own digital assets, off-internet page search engine optimization is all about enhancing your net web page's authority and relevance in the eyes of engines like google through strategies finished outdoor your net web page. This chapter objectives to get to the bottom of the complexities of off-internet web page seo and shed slight on the pivotal characteristic hyperlink constructing performs in advancing your internet web page's prominence and credibility in search engine rankings.

In the virtual technology wherein content material material is adequate, search engines like google and yahoo like Google have come to be extra discerning and complicated in figuring out the notable and relevance of internet pages. One critical way they look at this is with the useful resource of studying how one-of-a-kind web websites interact with yours. The not unusual experience is easy but profound: if an entire lot of super internet sites link on your internet web web page, it's far possibly that your content material is treasured and authoritative. Such out of doors indicators function endorsements, or votes of confidence, persuading search engines like google and yahoo like google to view your internet web site as a relied on beneficial resource deserving higher visibility.

This financial ruin will dissect the factors that constitute off-net page seo and the methodologies to build first-rate one-manner hyperlinks correctly. We'll additionally dive into know-how the significance of social alerts and the upward push of social media seek engine marketing, delving into the nuances of how social systems can circuitously effect your search engine overall performance. Additionally, this monetary disaster will provide insights into guest taking walks a blog and outreach strategies, an often unnoticed however pretty effective road for building valuable links and putting in place authority.

Subtopics protected on this monetary ruin will include:

6.1 Importance of Backlinks: Understand why oneway links are just like the foreign exchange of the internet, essential for putting in your website's authority.

6.2 Building High-Quality Backlinks: Learn the art and generation of building links that not best increase your ratings but additionally deliver in focused, excellent website online visitors.

6.Three Social Signals and Social Media search engine advertising: Explore the effect of social media interactions for your net website's SEO ordinary performance, and a way to leverage them for your advantage.

6.Four Guest Blogging and Outreach Strategies: Acquaint yourself with the strategies for crafting compelling vacationer posts and executing effective outreach campaigns that result in impactful one-way links.

By the give up of this monetary destroy, you may be equipped with actionable insights and examined strategies to raise your off-web page search engine marketing sport, turning you right into a seasoned digital marketer able to commanding every the on-internet page and rancid-net page elements critical for search engine optimization fulfillment. So, permit's embark on this adventure to decode the off-internet web page are seeking for engine advertising panorama and understand a way to efficaciously leverage it to create a robust and a long way-reaching on-line presence.

## 6.1. Importance of Backlinks

In the giant, interconnected internet of online records, oneway hyperlinks characteristic crucial pathways that manual serps and clients alike. If we don't forget a internet net site to be a virtual real belongings property, on the other hand hyperlinks are corresponding to the roads and highways that result in it. Not all roads are created identical; a few are nicely-paved, regular, and direct, on the identical time as others are treacherous and meandering. The same analogy applies to inbound hyperlinks—some are specifically precious, lending authority and credibility on your website, on the same time as others may be horrible, harming your web page's recognition or maybe incurring results from search engines like google like google.

## Chapter 10: The Concept Of Authority

One of the middle tenets of lower back-hyperlinks lies inside the idea of 'authority.' Search engines are in the business of presenting the most correct and relevant facts to customers. To try this, they need to evaluate the authority and credibility of a website. A excessive-authority net website online that links to your internet web page basically vouches on your content material, signaling to search engines like google and yahoo that your net page, too, should be taken into consideration authoritative. This "vote of self belief" dramatically complements your internet website's ability to rank higher in are looking for engine give up give up result pages (SERPs).

The Currency of the Web

You should consider back-hyperlinks due to the fact the 'foreign exchange' of the internet. They constitute a transaction of consider and authority, contributing cost not in truth to the recipient internet web website online however furthermore to the internet at massive. This mutual alternate can arise organically, which includes whilst a superb records website on-line references your research observe, or it can be engineered via strategic search engine optimization efforts, together with visitor posting or influencer outreach. Regardless of the technique, a robust one way link profile is essential for conducting high SERP rankings.

Quality Over Quantity

In the early years of seek engine marketing, the massive type of one-manner links was regularly taken into consideration the most crucial element for score. Sites may also need to amass plenty of links without plenty regard for the high-quality or relevance of these hyperlinks, principal to a skewed and with out troubles manipulated tool. However, search engines like google and yahoo have evolved drastically. Algorithms have emerge as an prolonged manner greater latest and now prioritize the top notch of oneway links over sheer numbers. A few incredible, relevant one way links from authoritative web websites can a ways outweigh the value of numerous low-quality, beside the point hyperlinks.

Anchor Text and Context

The terms used to link for your website, known as anchor textual content, deliver big weight in seek engine advertising. Well-optimized anchor textual content offers every clients and search engines like google like google and yahoo like google with easy context about the content cloth cloth of the link's holiday spot. However, over-optimizing anchor textual content with aggressive key-word targeting can bring about consequences. Hence, it's vital to hold a natural and sundry anchor text profile.

Relevance and Topical Authority

Beyond the idea of elegant authority, the relevance of a one-manner link also topics drastically. If your net website is focused on health and health, a one manner hyperlink from an amazing medical mag will deliver more weight than a link from an car blog. Search engines are increasingly emphasizing topical authority, in which the focus is on the specific state of affairs do not forget expertise exhibited with the aid of a website.

Do-Follow vs. No-Follow Links

In seo parlance, do-comply with hyperlinks pass on 'hyperlink juice,' contributing to the recipient internet internet website's authority, while no-look at links do now not. Originally, the no-follow characteristic changed into designed to combat unsolicited mail and discourage unethical hyperlink-building strategies. However, no-have a observe links can but contribute to a extra herbal-searching one-way link profile and strain treasured referral website site visitors.

Social Signals and Indirect Impact

Although social alerts like likes, stocks, and feedback on social media systems are not immediately counted as oneway hyperlinks, they frequently result in improved on line visibility and herbal one manner hyperlink opportunities. A blog positioned up that profits traction on social media would possibly possibly entice the attention of bloggers, newshounds, or influencers who can also then hyperlink to it, supplying treasured back-links now not without delay.

Risk of Penalties and the Importance of Monitoring

Bad links can damage you. Links from spammy internet web websites, or 'hyperlink farms,' can reason consequences from search engines. Therefore, ordinary monitoring of your one way hyperlink profile is essential. Tools like Google's Search Console or severa 1/three-party are searching for engine marketing and advertising and marketing structures can assist in this, presenting whole link analyses and bearing in mind the disavowal of unstable hyperlinks.

7. Local search engine optimization and Google My Business

In the virtual landscape, in which globalization appears to be the buzzword, the importance of localized focused on regularly takes a backseat. However, for companies that perform on a nearby scale or for worldwide entities searching out to goal specific areas, understanding the nuances of Local search engine optimization and Google My Business is essential. This monetary catastrophe objectives to offer an insightful investigate the area of Local search engine optimization, focusing especially on the instrumental feature completed via Google My Business in shaping close by are in search of outcomes.

Search engine optimization is not genuinely a one-duration-fits-all agency; it is a multifaceted location that adapts based totally mostly on various factors, which encompass the geographical area of your aim market. Local seo is the optimization approach for nearby are seeking for queries, regularly characterised with the aid of phrases like "near me," "in [City Name]," or "[Service] in [City]." The cause is to seem prominently in neighborhood search outcomes to seize the attention of nearby clients seeking out services or products that you provide.

Enter Google My Business (GMB)—Google's tool for coping with your enterprise corporation's online presence across its platform, particularly in Google Search and Google Maps. A well-optimized Google My Business listing can function a mini-net net web page of types, imparting capacity customers with critical facts like your employer hours, services, critiques, or maybe pics. For brick-and-mortar companies or company providers running inner specific geographical regions, Google My Business becomes an vital device for attracting footfall or generating close by leads.

In this bankruptcy, we're capable of deep-dive into the numerous factors that make Local seo and Google My Business so important for corporations running at the nearby diploma. Topics will encompass an outline of Local are trying to find engine marketing and advertising and marketing score factors, the nuts and bolts of putting in place and optimizing your Google My Business list, coping with on-line opinions, and the usage of specialized network searching for engine advertising tools for analytics. Each phase will provide actionable insights, expert recommendations, and strategic issues that would increase your local virtual presence, consequently using more site visitors—each on line and offline—for your company.

By the cease of this financial ruin, you need to have a entire expertise of a way to leverage Local seo and Google My Business as powerful equipment to your popular digital advertising and marketing technique. Whether you are a network mom-and-pop keep, a organization company, or a large agency with multiple places, the methods and techniques discussed right here is probably precious in connecting you with the neighborhood customers who're actively searching out the goods or services you provide.

Stay tuned as we get to the bottom of the complex tapestry of Local seo and Google My Business, elements that could very well be the missing portions to your digital advertising and marketing puzzle.

## 7.1. Local seek engine advertising Ranking Factors

The realm of Local seo is a microcosm inside the broader scope of seo, and it's miles abruptly evolving to deal with the changing behavior of clients. People often use search engines like google like google and yahoo to locate close by offerings, whether or not it's far a nearby cafe, a reliable plumber, or the first-rate hair salon in town. The query is, how do you're making your commercial enterprise stand out in local are searching for consequences? The solution lies in expertise and optimizing for Local search engine optimization rating elements.

The Significance of Local search engine advertising Ranking Factors

Local seek engine marketing rating factors are the unique variables that engines like google like google and yahoo use to determine the relevance and authority of a internet site or industrial organization listing for a localized seek query. Given the prevalence of smartphones, neighborhood are seeking out has become pretty famous; the term "close to me" has visible a large spike in usage, as an example. Therefore, know-how the metrics that have an effect on nearby ratings turns into essential for groups that carry out on a localized degree.

Local are looking for engine advertising isn't pretty a whole lot small companies catering to a selected locale; it is in addition applicable for large corporations with a couple of locations. This technique that every a mom-and-pop store and a national chain can leverage Local search engine marketing to electricity foot web site web page traffic to their establishments.

Key Local seek engine advertising Ranking Factors

While numerous elements make a contribution to close by scores, we are capable of delve into some of the maximum vital ones.

Google My Business (GMB) Optimization

The coronary heart and soul of any Local search engine optimization technique is a nicely-optimized Google My Business listing. The data you provide proper right here feeds right now into numerous Google offerings, consisting of Google Search and Google Maps. A surely finished and frequently updated GMB listing boosts your opportunities of performing inside the Google Local Pack, a hard and speedy of 3 highlighted Maps-based totally consequences offering the maximum pretty-rated and applicable organizations for a particular query.

To optimize your GMB list:

Ensure your business employer name, address, and speak to variety (NAP) are regular all through all structures.

Choose accurate classes that align together with your commercial organization.

Add brilliant pictures and videos to beautify person engagement.

Collect and control Google reviews (more on this later).

Website Localization

Localizing your website performs a pivotal function in resonating collectively together with your close by audience. This is going past mere translation in case you're running in a multilingual region. It consists of:

Using close by dialects and colloquialisms in your content material.

Featuring close by landmarks or activities relevant on your industrial business enterprise.

Adding neighborhood organisation schema markup to provide extra agency statistics to search engines like google and yahoo like google.

On-Page seo Factors

Your internet net page have to encompass crucial close by keywords, specifically in meta titles, headers, and content material material body. The NAP facts on your internet site ought to fit that of your GMB list. Ideally, every bodily location need to have a dedicated landing web web page optimized for nearby are seeking for.

# Chapter 11: User Engagement And Behavior

How clients engage together collectively along with your list and internet web page moreover influences your neighborhood rating. Google takes into consideration factors like:

Click-thru charge (CTR): The ratio of clients who click on in your list to folks that see it.

Bounce price: The percentage of website online traffic who navigate far from the internet site on-line after viewing best one web page.

Average time spent on the internet site on-line.

Reviews and Ratings

Online opinions and ratings are social proofs that now not most effective impact client options but furthermore impact close by seek scores. Google critiques are particularly critical for close by organizations. Encourage satisfied customers to leave exceptional opinions and usually reply to evaluations, whether or not powerful or horrible, because it indicates that you're engaged collectively with your customers.

Mobile Responsiveness

Most nearby searches stand up on mobile devices, making cellular optimization a key rating element. Google makes use of cellular-first indexing, because of this it commonly makes use of the cell model of a internet website for rating and indexing. A responsive, cell-exceptional internet site is critical for immoderate close by scores.

Advanced Considerations

Local seo may want to no longer save you at the factors listed above. As engines like google like google evolve, greater variables like voice searching for optimization, social indicators, or maybe augmented reality need to advantage prominence. Therefore, staying updated with the cutting-edge inclinations and continuously optimizing your method is important.

## 7.2. Google My Business Optimization

The Importance of Google My Business in Local search engine advertising

Google My Business (GMB) isn't always certainly every different list in the crowded digital universe; it is the nucleus of your local seek engine advertising and marketing and advertising technique. Often, GMB serves due to the fact the primary affect your corporation makes on potential clients searching on-line. Whether you are a comfortable neighborhood ebook shop, a close-by health club, or a multi-area restaurant chain, a properly-optimized GMB listing can be your charge tag to improved visibility, customer engagement, and foot internet site on line site visitors. While search engine optimization is a substantial concern, Local seo zeroes in on making your commercial organisation visible in community are seeking for results, and Google My

Business is the inspiration on which this visibility is constructed.

Getting Started with Google My Business

Creating a GMB list may also seem honest, but there are nuances to go through in mind if you purpose for superior widespread usual overall performance. To begin, visit the Google My Business net internet site and study the signal-up method, verifying your listing via postcard, cellphone, or email, depending to your kind of business enterprise and what options Google offers.

Key Elements of GMB Optimization

The significance of meticulously filling out each section of your GMB listing can not be overstated. Here's a breakdown of essential elements:

Business Name, Address, and Phone Number (NAP)

Your NAP information is crucial for local search score. Ensure that this facts is everyday at some point of all systems—your internet website, special on line listings, and social media. Inconsistencies can confuse Google's set of pointers and decrease your ranking.

Business Categories

Choosing the right enterprise classes helps Google determine which queries your list must seem for. Google lets in you to pick out a primary category and similarly instructions; pick those cautiously primarily based absolutely mostly on what your business offers.

Business Hours

Accurate company hours decorate person enjoy and can impact your community rankings. Google even allows for special hours to be set for holidays or particular events, so there is no excuse for wrong facts.

Photos and Videos

A photograph is well well worth one thousand terms, and within the context of GMB, likely even greater. High-incredible pics and movement photos not satisfactory make your list extra appealing but moreover provide insights into what clients can expect.

8. Content Marketing and search engine optimization

In the virtual advertising landscape, there are few disciplines as cautiously entwined as Content Marketing and Search Engine Optimization (seo). Individually, each represents a powerful mechanism for attracting audiences, building emblem credibility, and using business business enterprise targets. When mixed, but, the two create a synergistic effect that can extensively increase a brand's presence and effect on-line. This alliance among Content Marketing and seek engine advertising and advertising is neither unintended nor optional in ultra-contemporary exceptionally-aggressive digital surroundings. It is, alternatively, a crucial strategic alignment which can profoundly affect how efficiently organizations connect with their goal market in vast techniques.

Content Marketing is basically the paintings and era of creating precious, relevant material aimed now not at pitching your products or services, however at providing beneficial information or insights for your intention market. By turning in regular, super content material fabric, you could set up consider, nurture relationships, and ultimately, have an effect on behavior—regularly in the form of conversions or client loyalty.

On the opposite hand, search engine optimization is the complicated method of optimizing a website in order that it appears higher in are trying to find engine effects pages (SERPs). It's approximately know-how what human beings are trying to find online, the solutions they are looking for, the terms they're the usage of, and the content material they preference to devour. The surrender goal is to generate herbal visibility and location visitors from serps like google like google and yahoo.

Here's the synergy: High-wonderful content material cloth material is an asset that may be leveraged for are searching for engine advertising functions, and conversely, seo can channel a glide of centered, natural site visitors for your content material material material. This courting is on the identical time beneficial. Search engine optimization wishes content material to rank, and that content material becomes more valuable if it can be positioned with out difficulty by using way of the usage of the proper target audience, that's what search engine optimization accomplishes.

This section will delve into the nuanced techniques in which Content Marketing and search engine marketing intersect, assist, and extend every special. We'll talk how key-phrase studies informs content creation, how fantastic content material earns decrease lower back-hyperlinks, and how on-page optimization makes content extra effects discoverable through engines like google like google and yahoo. We'll additionally find out advanced topics together with semantic are looking for for, voice searching for, content material cloth clustering, and masses of others.

If you are trying to in fact draw near the digital arena, know-how the crucial courting between Content Marketing and seek engine advertising and marketing is fundamental. The next chapters will offer a entire framework for strategically integrating the ones disciplines, presenting a holistic approach to succeeding in cutting-edge-day day digital market.

eight.1. Content Strategy and Planning

In the big environment of on line marketing, content material fabric material acts because the nucleus spherical which orbits each top notch detail, be it seo, Social Media Marketing, PPC advertising and marketing and advertising and marketing, or each one-of-a-kind digital channel. Yet, creating extremely good content material with out a nicely-defined approach is similar to constructing a constructing with out blueprints: the forestall cease end result may be volatile, directionless, and no longer probable to stand up to the assessments of time and opposition. In this bankruptcy, we explore the pivotal feature of content material fabric method and planning in optimizing your seek engine advertising and marketing efforts, ensuring you are now not truly producing content material cloth fabric, however the 'right' content material cloth that serves every your audience and enterprise goals.

Why is Content Strategy Important?

Content technique isn't always quite a good deal what you'll create, however additionally why you're growing it, who you're developing it for, and the manner it fits into your broader corporation targets. It offers the framework that guarantees each piece of content material serves a selected cause and movements you nearer within the path of achieving your goals.

Imagine your commercial enterprise as a deliver. If seo is the sail that captures the wind, the content is the rudder that gives it direction. You can make investments all of the resources you have got into are looking for engine advertising and marketing, however without outstanding, strategically deliberate content material material fabric, those efforts may be useless in essential you in that you want to go.

The Role of seo in Content Strategy

seo acts as a guiding pressure in content cloth fabric approach. Once you recognize what your goal marketplace is attempting to find and the issues they're looking for to treatment, you can tailor your content material to meet the ones precise goals. Keyword studies isn't always pretty a lot locating terms to optimize for; it's far approximately gaining insights into the questions, issues, and goals of your audience. By aligning your content cloth technique with those insights, you are not best optimizing for search engines like google however also growing precious content material material that resonates together along with your goal market, thereby splendid each individual motive and are attempting to find algorithms' requirements for terrific.

Building a Content Calendar

One of the essential system in content making plans is the content fabric calendar. A nicely-idea-out content fabric material calendar permits you to:

Schedule content material cloth production and e-book

Keep track of key-word optimization

Align content material with seasonal traits or activities

Ensure consistency and fantastic

By mapping out your content material fabric manufacturing, you could higher allocate property, manipulate humans, and synchronize with extraordinary advertising and marketing and advertising and advertising sports activities. Your seo desires want to be carefully tied to this calendar, with key-word problems and goals set for every content material fabric piece.

The Four C's of Content Strategy

When planning your content material cloth method, do not forget the "Four Cs":

1.    Clarity: Your content should have a clear interest. What are the dreams? Are you seeking to train, tell, entertain, or convert?

2.    Consistency: Consistency is important in multiple dimensions—notable, style, tone, and publishing frequency. Inconsistent content material fabric fabric can erode acquire as actual with and undermine your search engine optimization efforts.

3. Creativity: searching for engine advertising isn't quite lots attractive algorithms. It's furthermore approximately delighting humans. Creative, compelling content material material is what maintains humans to your pages and encourages them to percent your content material, every of that might genuinely affect search engine optimization.

4. Conversion: Ultimately, the content material want to pressure motion. Whether it's far sharing the object, signing up for a book, or making a buy, every piece of content cloth material have to have a well-defined conversion goal that aligns together with your commercial organisation dreams.

Types of Content

Your content material fabric method want to consist of pretty some content material types to engage exquisite segments of your target audience at special degrees of the consumer's journey. These can range from weblog posts, prolonged-form articles, and case research to movies, podcasts, and infographics. Each type serves a totally unique reason and may be optimized for search engine optimization in fantastic methods.

Content Lifecycle and search engine optimization

Content isn't a difficult and speedy-it-and-overlook-it asset; it has a lifecycle. This lifecycle starts offevolved offevolved offevolved with ideation, observed via creation, optimization (for seo), ebook, advertising and advertising and marketing, commonplace normal performance tracking, and ultimately, updating or repurposing. Each diploma of the lifecycle offers possibilities for SEO optimization:

Ideation: Use search engine optimization keyword studies gadget for problem be counted technology.

Creation: Incorporate key phrases actually into your content cloth.

Optimization: Use metadata, HTML tags, and hooked up information.

Publication: Use seo-pleasant URLs and encompass inner hyperlinks.

Promotion: Use search engine advertising techniques for outreach and one manner link technology.

Performance Tracking: Use analytics to understand how well your content fabric is rating and changing.

Updating or Repurposing: Refresh previous content material material, and repurpose robust-performing content into special formats.

Measurement and KPIs

Your content material material strategy isn't always complete without metrics to evaluate its effectiveness. Key Performance Indicators (KPIs) like net page views, average time spent at the internet page, jump charge, and conversion expenses can offer insights into how nicely your content material cloth fabric is appearing and what additives require development. More superior KPIs must include scroll intensity, click on-thru costs (CTR) on internal links, or even unique engagement metrics like social shares or remarks.

eight.2.    Blogging for search engine advertising and marketing and marketing Success

Blogging has transcended its early fame as a trifling platform for non-public musings and diary-like entries. Today, it's an important device for agencies of all sizes and brands, now not great to hook up with clients but additionally as a cornerstone of any essential seo method. Blogs are rich soil in which you could cultivate an array of search engine marketing advantages — from driving natural site visitors and constructing logo authority to improving patron engagement and growing conversions. In this segment, allow's delve deep into why walking a weblog is a linchpin for seo success and the way you may grasp the art work of searching for engine advertising-extraordinary strolling a weblog.

The Intrinsic Connection Between Blogging and search engine optimization

One would possibly likely wonder why on foot a blog is so important to search around engine advertising and marketing and advertising and marketing while there are multiple channels to interest on, collectively with social media, PPC, and electronic mail advertising and marketing. The solution is twofold: content material material and relevance. Search engines thrive on new, applicable content fabric, and blogs are the most realistic and green techniques for companies to provide this content material. By continuously which include sparkling, high-quality content material material for your net net website online, you're not quality giving search engines like google greater reasons to index your pages however moreover offering treasured records that lets in remedy problems, tell choices, or entertain — thereby growing the probability of attracting and retaining your goal market.

## 9. Search engine optimization Analytics and Reporting

In the arena of Search Engine Optimization (search engine advertising), what gets measured receives controlled, and what gets controlled gets optimized. The significance of seo analytics and reporting can't be overstated because it sits at the intersection of information evaluation, overall performance tracking, and strategic making plans. As you assignment deeper into the labyrinth of search engine optimization—from gaining knowledge of on-web web page factors to crafting a bulletproof link-building approach—you could find that analytics and reporting act due to the fact the North Star guiding your efforts. These factors come up with the empirical proof you need to recognize how properly your strategies are walking and what modifications need to be made for reaching prolonged-time period achievement.

SEO analytics and reporting take you beyond the floor-level metrics. They provide deep insights into patron behavior, aggressive reputation, and marketplace traits. It's not quite tons knowing what number of human beings visited your net net web page or clicked on a link. It's approximately information the 'why' and 'how' in the returned of those numbers, which in turn, informs the 'what subsequent.' In a market this is ever-evolving, sturdy search engine optimization analytics and whole reporting can provide a aggressive facet that might make the difference amongst hovering in the rankings or disappearing into virtual oblivion.

In this phase, we are capable of delve into the requirements of search engine advertising analytics and reporting. We'll talk the severa metrics that depend, device that could useful resource in collecting and interpreting statistics, and pleasant practices for translating those insights into actionable techniques. From facts key performance signs (KPIs) to dissecting complicated analytics dashboards, we will offer a detailed roadmap for studying this pivotal element of seo. Whether you're a newbie dipping your toes into the hunt engine advertising and marketing pool or a seasoned expert searching for to improve your analytics sport, this manual targets to characteristic a entire beneficial aid.

By the give up of this exploration, you could respect that seo isn't always in reality an artwork however a technological statistics, underpinned with the resource of quantitative statistics and qualitative insights. Welcome to the world of seo Analytics and Reporting—in which information drives alternatives, and alternatives force success.

## 9.1. Google Analytics for search engine advertising

In the quest engine marketing panorama, Google Analytics stands as a vital device for tracking, measuring, and reading your website's ordinary overall performance. Over the years, Google Analytics has developed into a sturdy platform that gives valuable insights into now not genuinely quantitative metrics like pageviews or jump costs however moreover qualitative factors like consumer behavior and interaction. The tool is, in essence, your window into information how traffic are interacting along with your website, what content cloth they discover treasured, and wherein there are bottlenecks on your individual revel in that can be hurting your seek engine marketing efforts.

# Chapter 12: Google Analytics Is Indispensable

bolts, permit's recognize why Google Analytics is taken into consideration a linchpin for any seek engine advertising and marketing method. First and essential, Google Analytics permits you show screen your internet website on line's normal performance in real-time. This allows you to be agile, making brief changes to your content material or layout and searching at the instantaneous effect on metrics. Secondly, the device permits you place and display Key Performance Indicators (KPIs) which might be aligned together with your business agency dreams, providing you with a measurable scale in competition to which to decide your search engine advertising techniques. Thirdly, Google Analytics allows you to advantage target market insights, presenting you with data on demographics, hobbies, and behavior, which you could leverage to intention your seo techniques more effectively. Last however no longer least, Google Analytics is intently blanketed with certainly one of a type Google services, along with Google Search Console and Google Ads, providing a entire atmosphere for your digital advertising and marketing efforts.

Setting Up Google Analytics

For rookies, the gadget begins with installing location Google Analytics for your internet web site. This involves growing an account and which incorporates a completely unique tracking code to your net net web page's codebase. Once that is finished, Google Analytics will start collecting data out of your net website online, presenting you the possibility to dissect this statistics in diverse techniques. There are severa guides and tutorials to be had on line that will help you in installing region Google Analytics. Make high-quality to also set up dreams, which may be particular interactions or benchmarks you need customers to complete, consisting of making a purchase, filling out a touch form, or spending a extremely good amount of time on a selected web web page.

Key Metrics to Monitor

While Google Analytics gives a large variety of metrics, focusing on the ones which can be most relevant for your are looking for engine advertising overall performance is critical. Some of those key metrics include:

1.	Organic Traffic: This shows the type of website site visitors coming in your internet website online via search engines like google and is a primary degree of your search engine advertising and advertising achievement.

2.	Bounce Rate: This represents the share of unmarried-net page visits in which the customer leaves with out interacting with the internet web page. A immoderate bounce rate might also additionally advise that your landing pages aren't convincing sufficient to customers, or the content cloth is not what the traveller anticipated.

3.     Page Load Time: Slow loading pages create a horrible purchaser experience and can negatively effect your are trying to find engine rankings.

4.     User Behavior: Under the Behavior tab, you can discover how customers are interacting together together with your net net page, what pages they go to most usually, and the way prolonged they live on the ones pages. This records may be useful for content optimization.

5.     Conversion Rate: If your internet web page has a particular call-to-motion (like developing a purchase or signing up for a guide), the conversion price shows you the percentage of finished goals towards the entire web page traffic.

6.     User Flow: This metric visualizes the path customers take thru your internet site online and wherein they drop off. This can highlight complicated regions to your navigation or funnel.

## Advanced Features: Segmentation and Custom Reporting

One of the handiest capabilities of Google Analytics is the capability to create custom segments and opinions. Segmentation allows you to isolate and analyze precise subsets of your information. For example, you could create a segment of customers who visited a particular page after which completed a particular motion. Custom reviews will allow you to create tailored opinions that show first-class the metrics and dimensions you care about, introduced straight away to your inbox at ordinary intervals.

### Integrating with Google Search Console

For an extra layer of perception, Google Analytics can be blanketed with Google Search Console, each different valuable device for seo. This integration lets in you to view Search Console facts like clicks, impressions, and common ranking function right away in the Google Analytics interface. By combining this facts with the wealthy customer metrics furnished thru Google Analytics, you could have a properly-rounded know-how of each how clients discover your website in search and what they do when they get there.

Limitations and Ethical Considerations

While Google Analytics offers a wealth of records, it's critical to be aware that it is no longer simply accurate. Cookie blockers, VPN utilization, and unique privateness tool can intrude with information collection. Additionally, moral troubles concerning client privateness and records protection have to not be neglected. Make certain to conform with privacy felony tips like GDPR and be apparent with clients approximately the statistics you acquire.

nine.2. Search engine optimization Metrics and Key Performance Indicators

SEO (Search Engine Optimization) is an ever-evolving assignment, and its efficacy is predicated upon on severa variables, a number of which are out of your manage. However, what is interior your control is the way you degree achievement and adjust your techniques as a result. This is wherein are seeking for engine marketing metrics and Key Performance Indicators (KPIs) come into play. These metrics and signs and symptoms are essential in supplying a quantifiable diploma of your internet site's performance. By maintaining a near eye on specific KPIs, you can glean insights that strain knowledgeable alternatives, assisting you refine your search engine marketing strategies for optimum tremendous outcomes.

What Are search engine optimization Metrics and Why Are They Important?

search engine advertising and marketing metrics are measurable values that display the effectiveness of your search engine optimization efforts. These metrics help you understand whether or not your seek engine marketing strategies are jogging as meant or need changes. In essence, they will be essential remarks mechanisms. Without them, it's like crusing a deliver without a compass—you don't have any way to decide in case you are heading inside the right path.

The Significance of Key Performance Indicators (KPIs)

KPIs are unique, predetermined metrics that align cautiously together collectively together with your commercial enterprise company dreams. While the phrases 'metrics' and 'KPIs' are frequently used interchangeably, it's miles essential to differentiate amongst them. All KPIs are metrics, but no longer all metrics are KPIs. KPIs are metrics that are most intently tied to employer goals and consequently require particular interest.

10. E-Commerce search engine optimization

In present day-day digitally interconnected worldwide, the battle for client interest has moved from billboards and tv monitors to search around engine end result pages (SERPs). As e-exchange keeps to develop exponentially, the competition amongst on line stores has in no way been more fierce. This changing panorama has brought seo (Search Engine Optimization) to the primary edge of virtual techniques for e-exchange corporations, massive and small. Welcome to the complex, dynamic, and fairly profitable international of E-Commerce seo.

The journey of a purchaser—from a informal browser to a loyal consumer—is often more complex than we recognise. It starts offevolved inside the extensive ocean of online statistics, in which the patron is but a click away from an array of options. Here, visibility is essential. A business that can not be without trouble determined is much like a storefront in a desolate alley. Search engine optimization serves because the guiding moderate that leads customers through this elaborate maze, immediately in your digital storefront.

But what precisely is E-Commerce seo, and the way does it vary from traditional seo? At its middle, E-Commerce seo features a tough and speedy of optimizations and techniques geared in the direction of improving a web keep's visibility in search engines like google. However, the programs, stressful situations, and techniques specific to E-Commerce seek engine advertising and marketing are frequently extra complicated and specialised. Product listings, magnificence pages, customer evaluations, and a multitude of different factors come into play, every with its precise search engine advertising and marketing troubles.

E-Commerce seo isn't always pretty loads the use of web site visitors; it is about using licensed internet web page web page site visitors. It's approximately ensuring that the people who arrive at your on line maintain are individuals who are actively looking for the goods you promote. This optimization transcends the traditional obstacles of search engine optimization, intermingling with components of consumer enjoy, content material approach, or perhaps stock manipulate.

The importance of reading E-Commerce search engine optimization is large. Not handiest does it effect your net web page's rankings in search engine consequences, however it right away correlates with conversion costs, purchaser retention, and profits era. An effective E-Commerce search engine marketing method can propose the distinction amongst a thriving corporation and a shuttered on-line keep. As the e-trade organisation evolves, search engine advertising and marketing and advertising stays a regular variable inside the equation for achievement, adapting to new algorithms, technologies, and consumer behaviors.

In the subsequent sections, we are going to find out the numerous aspects of E-Commerce seek engine advertising, from key-phrase research and on-web web page optimization to technical issues and past. Whether you're an search engine advertising newbie or a seasoned veteran, there can be normally room to refine your method, find out new avenues, and preserve up with the ever-changing algorithms that dictate the recommendations of the sport.

So, permit's embark on this adventure to demystify E-Commerce search engine optimization and release the overall capability of your online keep. It's time to turn searches into income, browsers into customers, and clicks into loyal clients. Welcome to the future of exchange; welcome to E-Commerce search engine optimization.

## 10.1. Search engine optimization for E-Commerce Websites

search engine advertising for E-Commerce internet web sites gives a very precise set of challenges and possibilities that differentiate it extensively from seo for blogs, informational net websites, or business enterprise internet web sites. Online shops characteristic in a rather aggressive panorama, jostling for the excessive spots on are seeking for engine results pages (SERPs) now not exceptional in opposition to distinct e-commerce websites but additionally toward informational net net web sites, evaluation web sites, and extra. That's why information the precise nuances of seek engine advertising and marketing for E-Commerce web websites is critical for all people in search of to go into this competitive marketplace.

## Chapter 13: A Multi-Dimensional Approach

One vital thing to be privy to E-Commerce seek engine marketing is its multi-dimensional nature. Unlike a weblog, in which you could amazing fear approximately optimizing articles or touchdown pages, an e-alternate net internet site has numerous kinds of pages—homepages, class pages, product pages, and additional. Each type of web page calls for a tailored search engine marketing method.

Homepages: This is typically the most authoritative internet page on an e-exchange internet website on-line. You'll want to optimize it for broader industry key terms and offer a easy, concise navigation menu to funnel customers to precise elements of the net internet site on line. Having a nicely-primarily based homepage gadgets the tone for search engine optimization fulfillment for the duration of the rest of the internet site on-line.

Category Pages: These are the bread and butter of your search engine optimization efforts. When customers search for big terms like "women's shoes" or "smartphones," they're commonly directed to beauty pages. Optimizing those pages includes right key-word studies, on-internet net web page seo, and strategic inner linking.

Product Pages: These are arguably the maximum challenging to optimize. Since you can have hundreds or masses of product pages, automation and template optimization come to be crucial. You'll need to avoid duplicate content material problems, ensure that each internet web page has a very unique meta description and pick out out, and include schema markup to reveal rich snippets.

Keyword Strategy: Beyond the Basics

Keywords in e-trade are not quite much locating excessive-quantity are in search of terms. They additionally want to be quite applicable to the product or magnificence you are promoting. Relevance enables not truly in score but moreover in conversion, this is the surrender intention.

For example, in case you're selling immoderate-give up wristwatches, a keyword like "low fee watches" also can moreover have immoderate searching for volume but isn't possibly to convert nicely on your merchandise. Here, prolonged-tail key phrases which incorporates "highly-priced wristwatches for guys" or "top rate women's gold watches" may additionally moreover offer much less visitors but higher conversion prices.

Content is Still King

Even even though you're strolling a web maintain, content is still critical for search engine optimization achievement. Product descriptions, critiques, or maybe weblog posts relevant in your enterprise can function precious content fabric.

Product Descriptions: Unique and specific product descriptions no longer most effective assist in score however moreover offer the purchaser with valuable information, which may be a decisive aspect in finishing a buy.

Reviews: Customer reviews upload unique content material to the net web page and moreover impact score. A web page with a excessive amount of top notch evaluations is probably to rank higher than a comparable web web page with out them. Reviews additionally make contributions to the richness of key terms on a web web page, often which include applicable extended-tail key phrases without any guide intervention.

Blogs: Adding a blog section allow you to rank for brought keywords that won't naturally wholesome into your product or class pages. Blog posts moreover offer an tremendous opportunity for internal linking, in addition boosting the search engine optimization of key coins pages.

Technical search engine advertising and marketing Considerations

E-Commerce internet web sites regularly be stricken with the useful resource of technical search engine marketing troubles because of their complicated form. Issues like slow load time, non-responsive layout, or insufficient cell optimization can all have an impact in your seek engine ratings.

Page pace is a crucial difficulty, mainly in the age of cell surfing. Slow-loading web web sites now not handiest deter capacity clients but are also penalized with the aid of the usage of using search engines like google. Employing techniques like lazy loading for pics, optimizing code, and leveraging browser caching can dramatically decorate site tempo.

Mobile optimization is not optionally available. With Google's cellular-first indexing, your net web page's cellular version is what gets listed and ranked. Therefore, having a mobile-responsive format is crucial.

Security and User Experience

Search engines prioritize internet internet sites that offer a steady and seamless character revel in. An SSL certificates is a should for any e-trade internet internet page. Not quality does it steady the transaction manner, but Google furthermore offers a moderate rating increase to HTTPS web web sites.